YOUR LIFE IS A BOOK

YOUR LIFE IS A BOOK

HOW TO CRAFT & PUBLISH YOUR MEMOIR

Brenda Peterson and Sarah Jane Freymann

SASQUATCH BOOKS
SEATTLE

*To the memory of my mother, Nita Florence. The older
I get, the more I appreciate her courage and dignity.*
—SARAH JANE FREYMANN

For my inspiring students, who are also my teachers.
—BRENDA PETERSON

Printed in the United States of America
Published by Sasquatch Books

18 17 16 15 14   9 8 7 6 5 4 3 2 1

Editor: Gary Luke
Project editor: Michelle Hope Anderson
Cover design: Briar Levit
Cover photograph: Lisa Warninger
Interior design: Anna Goldstein
Copy editor: Elizabeth Johnson

Library of Congress Cataloging-in-Publication Data is available.

ISBN: 978-1-57061-930-4

Sasquatch Books
1904 Third Avenue, Suite 710
Seattle, WA 98101
(206) 467-4300
www.sasquatchbooks.com
custserv@sasquatchbooks.com

Brenda Peterson's "An Author's Guide to Publishing," May 30, 2013,
and "Occupy the Book," October 26, 2011, were originally published
in the *Huffington Post* and adapted here.

Certified Chain of Custody
SUSTAINABLE   Promoting Sustainable Forestry
FORESTRY
INITIATIVE   www.sfiprogram.org
              SFI-01268

SFI label applies to the text stock

Be yourself—everybody else is taken.

~**OSCAR WILDE**

CONTENTS

USER'S GUIDE

With this book, we hope to help you write the best memoir possible from the often confusing, exhilarating, and unexpected raw material of your life. Between us—Brenda Peterson and Sarah Jane Freymann—we are writer, memoirist, teacher, and literary agent.

Brenda is the author of more than eighteen books; she has gained insights through a long career as a writing teacher and by publishing two memoirs—*Build Me an Ark: A Life with Animals* and *I Want to Be Left Behind: Finding Rapture Here on Earth*. Brenda has taught private writing classes in Seattle for two decades and delights in seeing many of her students published.

Sarah Jane is a New York City literary agent who has shepherded books onto best-seller lists, mentored fledgling writers, and helped authors transform their lives through memoir.

We have also taught memoir writing seminars together on the East and West Coasts. From our decades of experience, we can say with absolute certainty that every life is remarkable, rich, and amazing in its own way. But the story of those lives has to be well told if it's to yield a book others will want to read. That is the mission of *Your Life Is a Book*.

Whether you're writing for self-exploration, to leave a legacy, or for publication, we'll take you on a step-by-step journey from concept to completion. We've structured this book for accessibility and exploration. Part 1 is "Crafting Your Memoir" and Part 2 is "Getting Serious about Publishing." In each chapter, we share with you our knowledge of both how to write memoir and how to

> *A memoir is like a love story, with all the ecstasies, disappointments, and turning points of any relationship.*

bring it to what editors call its "brightest light." We also tell real-life stories of other authors whose memoirs have transformed their life and work.

At the end of each chapter, we offer writing prompts, as well as practical publishing tips, which will help you decide which audience you want to reach: private or public. For those of you who are intent on publishing your memoir, Part 2 guides you through the real-world business of traditional and indie publishing.

How you use this book is entirely up to you. Our advice is to read *Your Life Is a Book* from beginning to end, so you can build your book on the solid ground that it has taken us years to discover. But you may choose to first review the chapter headings and sample the content that interests you most. For example, if you are writing a travel memoir based on a spiritual journey, you might begin with Chapter 7, "Eat, Pray, Love," and then Chapter 8, "Travel Memoirs: Journeys In and Out," and then Chapter 11, "Spiritual Memoirs." That would give you the foundation for your narrative arc.

You could then read the other chapters to learn such vital elements as characterization, setting, dialogue, and building epiphanies, so the reader can share in your hard-won wisdom. Because that's what a memoir is all about: giving to your readers the pleasures, dramas, and insights from your unique life story. We hope that in this book you'll discover how writing your memoir adds another dimension to your life.

Good readers await you. And we're with you every step. So begin the work!

PART 1

CRAFTING YOUR MEMOIR

And the day came when the risk to remain tight in a bud
was more painful than the risk it took to blossom.

~ANAÏS NIN

A memoir is like a love story, with all the ecstasies, disappointments, and turning points of any relationship. And at the end, you might be surprised to discover that the love of your life is—your life.

Your memoir will open doorways to yourself and the world: to acceptance, awareness, and fulfillment. In memoir, we come home to ourselves and ultimately realize that life makes sense. And with this realization often comes the happiness of true understanding. Memoir is always a search for self, and *everyone's* personal story is rich in drama, relationships, and surprising discoveries. Yet nobody comes to us and says, "I'm writing a book about myself." They'll say, "This is a search for family roots, my homeland, and lost relatives," or, "This book is about surviving illness and finally finding happiness." Those may be the main themes and characters in your story, but ultimately, every memoir has one main theme— your evolution as a person. And one main character—you. This is the drama that drives the book. The question of a memoir is not just, "Who am I?" but "Who am I in *this* story?"

Often it's not what you expect that makes your story remarkable. Perhaps it *is* your achievements, your travels, or your philosophies. But maybe it's something simple and familiar that you've just taken for granted, something hidden in the background that emerges only as you reflect upon your life.

Best-selling memoirist Sy Montgomery, Sarah Jane's longtime author, found her life story in her own backyard with an endearing pig named Christopher Hogwood. Sy has traveled the world writing about animals—from Amazon pink dolphins to Sumatran tigers, but Sarah Jane finally convinced her to write about life with her charismatic pig. This huge, cheerful "Buddha master," taught Sy lessons in self-acceptance, extended family, and the value of community. Christopher Hogwood even taught Sy to be more human. Her memoir, *The Good Good Pig*, concludes with the understanding that many of us long for: "One thing I know for sure: a great soul can appear among us at any time, in the form of any creature. I'm keeping my eyes open."

So much of memoir is simply keeping your eyes open. The most engaging memoirs are not "facts-on-file" records of life dramas—but vivid details of the *where* and *what* and *how*. In the twentieth century, memoir edged out fiction as the most popular literary form—and that trend endures into the twenty-first century. Happily, memoir is no longer the exclusive province of celebrities or those whose fame is their sole credential. The fad of publishing just celebrity memoirs—celebrity wisdom would fill a very thin volume—is being replaced by what we call "the egalitarian memoir." The story of how everyday people survive the loss of a child, an illness, a search for a homeland, or a life-changing romance can be as compelling as a famous person's autobiography. And certainly more authentic. In memoirs, we now turn to our peers to learn better how to live.

Brenda's student, Claire Dederer, wrote a hugely popular memoir about balancing her daily life as mother and writer. Her book, *Poser: My Life in Twenty-Three Yoga Poses*, shows how an "ordinary" life, well told, is resonant for many readers. Claire, who came of age in the turbulent and exhilarating 1970s, first created fictional sketches based on her family—a feminist, free-spirited mother and two fathers. As Claire explored her own voice, a witty, irreverent memoirist emerged to observe the anxieties and pleasures of her own generation of women and mothers—all woven into her fledgling yoga practice.

Reflecting on your life can hold a secret healing in the present. When Sarah Jane was first approached to represent Jarvis

Jay Masters, a prisoner on death row, she declined to read the manuscript. But several Buddhist friends persuaded her to take another look at his handwritten pages. As she did, she entered into a world that, while painful, was redemptive. Jarvis's memoirs, *Finding Freedom: Writings from Death Row* and *That Bird Has My Wings: The Autobiography of an Innocent Man on Death Row*, are a testament to honesty, forgiveness, and inherent goodness. By telling his story, Jarvis finds spaciousness in solitary confinement and humor in the darkness of prison. As he says, "Writing and meditating saved my life."

Clearly, while we're all part of families and communities, we often feel like Jarvis, like we're in solitary confinement. Telling our stories as if for the first time, but with a deep sense of recognition and understanding, helps us realize we are not alone. We also discover a range of being as we create characters of others and ourselves.

Sometimes life stories are terribly sad, other times wonderfully funny. And often, they're both. Brenda discovered halfway through writing her second memoir that she was not a tragic heroine—a victim of Southern fundamentalism—but rather a comic, picaresque character. As her writing mentor, novelist and literary critic Diane Johnson, first taught her, "Pain . . . plus time . . . equals comedy."

When you tell your story, an extraordinary universe is revealed. As a mature person encountering a younger self, you change. Past experiences, even poignant ones, enrich the present, because you are not simply observing and reporting—you are participating in reliving. If you've ever had any doubts about your life's true purpose, writing your story will help you discover it.

1.
START ANYWHERE

When you wake up, you notice that you're here.
~ANNIE DILLARD, "TO FASHION A TEXT"

The memoirist must always find a way to begin her story, but memory is never chronological. So as Sarah Jane advises her authors, "Start anywhere. Because no matter where you start, you'll end up where you're meant to be." You might not have realized it yet, but your journey has already begun. Maybe you haven't written it down, yet you've been telling stories most of your life. Now, you just need to make the transition from your head to your hand.

One of the things we find very helpful is to actually ritualize this movement by making a space for your writing and finding elegant and enjoyable tools to help you. Remember your first day of school as a child? You delighted in buying new back-to-school supplies: notebooks, fabulous pens, maybe a new backpack or, these days, a laptop. Draw on this sense of excitement and anticipation now as a memoirist, as you get ready to go not back to school but back to your life.

Go to an art store for supplies. Or get a contact high from the manic learning curve at your local Apple or PC store. Enjoy the excitement of preparation and anticipation by allowing yourself to buy some really "special effects" for writing. So much is made of the pain of writing memoir, but there is also real pleasure. And working with beautiful tools is a good beginning.

Just as you must nurture your imagination as an artist, you must also nurture your writing space. You might be perfectly content at the kitchen table with children clamoring and phones ringing. In fact, one of Brenda's successful students, Gail Hudson, who is now coauthoring books with primatologist Jane Goodall, did a lot of her mental work in the kitchen. But she trained her children to realize that she was writing, and that she shouldn't be disturbed, even when she wasn't in her study.

Gail tells the story of standing at the stove stirring homemade spaghetti sauce as she ruminated over a chapter. Her young son was demanding her attention, but her older daughter interrupted his shouts.

"Quiet!" she reminded him. "Can't you see that Mom is writing?"

When the scene she'd contemplated over spaghetti sauce was finally vivid in her mind, Gail went to her study and wrote it all down.

Your writing room is not just decor or convenience; it's a kind of shrine. If you think of a memoir as a pilgrimage and yourself as a traveler, then the moment you cross the threshold into your writing room, you begin your journey.

Start anywhere. Because no matter where you start, you'll end up where you're meant to be.

A SHRINE OR AN ALTAR FOR YOUR MEMOIR

Envision your shrine as a visible representation of your journey. The objects you place there represent the steps you take. With each new chapter you will want to find the object that best represents your next discovery. Some shrines can be extraordinarily elaborate. Others are simpler, even austere. Make yours a personal expression of who you are and where you are in the moment.

Because Sarah Jane is in the process of renovating her New York City workspace, she has had to rethink her shrine. Having just taken a class in making terrariums, it occurred to her that she could create a charming little shrine that would happily sit inside her glass tank on her desk by the window. She lined the bottom with stones upon which she placed various objects that have special meaning for her: green moss, seashells, a small statue, a Tibetan Buddhist bell, a silly little charm from a bracelet her daughter wore when she was little. All these objects are inspiration for her writing journey.

One of Brenda's students asked her husband to build a small tree house in the backyard for her writing. He did, with a bookshelf, a writing desk, and a picture window with a view of their garden. There, she wrote three books that were later published. Some of Brenda's students take writing retreats together to rustic coastal cabins. They plan their writing time, their critique time, and their playtime together. It has made for a marvelous and very productive experience. And if you bring others, you can share the expenses.

Brenda and journalist Laura Shapiro worked together on their individual books over several years. Brenda was writing her novel *Duck and Cover*, and Laura was at work on her first book, *Perfection Salad: Women and Cooking at the Turn of the Century*. Every week they met at a Seattle coffee shop, The Daily Grind. Upon entering it, ideas and constructive critiques seemed to flow as easily as espresso, and they brainstormed solutions to their writing blocks.

But when Laura hit a major snag in her work, she realized that she needed a new workspace—she needed to literally create a holding space for her words before they could be allowed to leave her head. So Laura rented an office outside her home. Every day, the ritual of riding the bus downtown gave her the transition and pilgrimage time she needed. Inside the safety of her office, like a shrine or sanctuary, Laura could let her words flow. *Perfection Salad* was a critical success and is still in print thirty years later. The book established Laura as a major food critic and writer. It was followed by other wonderful books, including *Something from the Oven: Reinventing Dinner in 1950s America* and *Julia Child: A Life.*

WHAT IS YOUR PROCESS?

More important than where to start is discovering your writing process and how you learn about the world. Because that will determine how you create a book about your life. In teaching and working with writers, we've discovered that each person has a different process, and that a writer may or may not be aware of her process.

When Brenda was at the *New Yorker* working with fiction editor Rachel MacKenzie, there was another young writer at the magazine who was often quite ill. Rachel noted with her usual candor, "Oh, that's simply her writing process. Megan learns about life through illness."

Every writer has different triggers, muses, and ways of knowing their worlds. You'll have a head start on your book if you can figure out how you've learned your life lessons. Through illness? Through travel and play? Through the natural world and animals? Through trauma and drama? Through research? Intimacy? Relationships? Work? Search for roots? Spiritual search?

Identifying your own process will help you more consciously create your life story. For many writers, it is only by writing their life story that they begin to see the patterns of how they process and learn about life. One of Sarah Jane's authors learns about life through throwing herself into exotic settings and surviving strange encounters with wild animals; another uses food as a lens to better witness and make sense of the world around him. Another has found spiritual freedom while serving out a life sentence on death row.

And whatever your process, never forget your audience. This is where the craft comes in. When you make meaning of what might, at the time, seem senseless, it keeps the reader involved—we can hardly wait to experience what the writer will learn next. So the plot of any memoir is not just "What happens next?" It's what more you've discovered about yourself and the world around you.

A spiritual teacher once told Brenda that if you were to look at your life from the end to the beginning, you'd realize that everything that happened was for a purpose and provided you with what you needed to learn. That's why in both of Brenda's memoirs she starts midlife and then flashes back to her childhood. This strategy lets the reader know she has survived and arrived at a place of some self-understanding before showing how she got here.

THE DARK FAMILY SECRET

Sometimes your dark family secret is the force that sets the story in motion, the impetus that will unleash or jump-start your own writing. During her memoir class, Sarah Jane was grappling with her own family secret, the origins of which, in a convoluted way, dated back to World War II. After a while, it occurred to her that every family was hiding at least one dark secret, and even though its origins sometimes went back several generations, its power could still hold sway, affecting family dynamics to this day.

At first, her students were amused when she gave them the assignment to write on this subject—then they were baffled.

Surely if their family were harboring such a secret, they protested, it would have surfaced by now. Nonetheless, Sarah Jane urged them to write. In their follow-up essays, these students, with whom she had been working for over a year, revealed the most astounding stories: suicide, murder, illegitimate children, and ways in which generations-old money determined who currently wielded power. Those secrets had either been so hidden or so ingrained in the fabric of the students' lives that even though they had revealed all kinds of intimate details in previous assignments, it had never occurred to them to consider *the* dark secret. Writing about it revealed a world of truths, brought to light a previously hidden family mystery, and opened the door to new levels of insight and storytelling.

Exercise: Fill Out This Questionnaire

1) What is your best time of day to write? When are you most alert and present? Keep a chart of these times and write then.

2) Where is your most creative space to write? Do you need "a place of your own"?

3) Who can support you as a kind of bodyguard to keep your writing time sacred? Your partner? A friend? Siri?

4) How long can you go without reading a text, checking e-mail, or answering your phone?

5) How much anxiety do you feel when you unplug? Can you ease that somehow?

6) How will you reward yourself in small and simple ways when you succeed in creating writing time and space?

7) How can you expand your attention span to have greater access to your subconscious, your memories, and your life?

0) What is your process of the way you learn most about life?

9) Like a shaman, what is the gift you bring back to others from your own journey?

10) What is your dark family secret?

Exercise: Make a Schedule

When are you the most creative? Mornings, nights, middle of the night? Set up your schedule so that you can give that most precious time to your writing practice. David Guterson wrote *Snow Falling on Cedars* in the very early morning before he had to teach high school. Another best-selling author discovered that if she set her alarm for 3:00 a.m. and wrote until 6:00 a.m., she could finish a book in a year.

On your calendar, block out times each week for writing and exercising. Be sure to include resting, recess, or downtime. Stick to this schedule yourself and also engage your family and friends to help you honor these routines. Many writers work at home with huge distractions and people around who don't realize they are "at work." One of our author friends actually announces her "daily writing retreats" on her voice-mail message so that callers will understand that she is inaccessible during those hours. People will soon get the picture and respect your schedule.

One way to make sure you get your proper exercise is by finding a workout pal for the gym, walks, running—whatever exercise works for you. Many times that friend will help you stay on schedule when you might otherwise lapse. As for naps, one of our favorite authors, Diane Ackerman, author of *A Natural History of the Senses*, recommends "spanieling." Imagine you're a cocker spaniel, she suggests; find a cozy corner and lazily relax with "doglike dereliction."

Since memory is a memoirist's canvas, seek out ways to enhance your memory and mental alertness. Brenda plays a game with her students to help them access their memories: it's called "Open the Door."

Close your eyes. Imagine you are in a deep cave and walking down seven stone steps. There is a door at the bottom of the steps that is locked. Breathe fully into your chest and belly with each step and slowly exhale. Know that when you reach that door, there will be someone or some memory awaiting you. All you have to do is open that door and a story is there. It has always been waiting for you to find it again. Write that story.

Writing Prompts

I have survived _____ because of my _____.

It was not until my encounter with _____ that I understood _____.

After my experiences with [loss, sickness, broken heart, abuse, betrayal], I finally "got it." I recognized that I learned most when I was _____.

PUBLISHING TIPS

Many of the rules change if you actually want to publish your memoir. Be practical. Think ahead. Set some publishing goals that are realistic. Do you plan an indie or self-publication with complete artistic control, or have you always dreamed of a traditional publisher? The invaluable magazine *Poets & Writers* offers contests, articles for aspiring authors, and great interviews with successful writers. We suggest that you also read other people's memoirs and study the structure of their books, as we do in this guide. Check out the agents and editors they acknowledge. Keep a list of these editors and agents for your future submissions.

As you read other memoirs, consider whether the author tells the story chronologically or thematically. Do they start in the present and flash back to childhood, as both of Brenda's memoirs do? Or does your favorite memoir focus on one specific time period, like the World War II Germany in Anne Frank's *Diary of a Young Girl*? Connect to your own personal history by setting your story in a historical context.

Is there a setting or drama that recurs in your memoir? A historical event? Read history and other memoirs set in the same time period as your own life. If you are writing to be published, keep the image of an ideal reader in your mind. Always remember that a companionable stranger is reading your memoir. Someone who will benefit from all the time and hard work you've put into this life story. You may start anywhere. But if you want to publish, you must always keep the reader in mind.

2.

FOLLOW
THE THREAD

While you hold it you can't get lost . . .
You don't ever let go of the thread.
~WILLIAM STAFFORD, "THE WAY IT IS"

Let's say that by now you've created time, a space, and a longer attention span for your memoir to flourish. You are writing memories and scenes in no particular order, with the intent of simply generating material. When you create stories, they are always in search of an organizing principle, or narrative arc, often without our knowing. Think of these scenes as quilt pieces in search of a pattern—what will become a story quilt.

QUILT PIECES IN SEARCH OF A PATTERN

Unless quilters begin with a design format, they know that sooner or later they'll have enough pieces to figure one out. When you write nonlinear scenes, a pattern may not be readily apparent, but you can sometimes sense a kind of organizing intelligence at work, or the hint of a pattern. This is your subconscious, and you should trust it as you would a lifeline. As Apple's Steve Jobs said

> *Think of your scenes as quilt*
> *pieces in search of a pattern.*

in a Stanford University commencement speech, "You can't connect the dots looking forward; you can only connect them looking
backward. So you have to trust that the dots will somehow connect in your future."

Who is connecting all of these dots? There is the famous story
of a Stanford psychology professor who hypnotized a woman to
illustrate a point to his class. He asked the woman to sink her
elbow into a glass of ice water for several minutes. Under hypno-
sis, the woman easily withstood the extreme cold.

"You see," the professor explained to his graduate students,
"she feels no pain."

One of the curious students asked, "Doesn't some part of her
feel pain?"

"No," the professor answered firmly.

Then came the eerie, disembodied voice of the hypnotized
woman herself. "I do," she said. "I feel the pain."

"Who are you?" the professor asked, confounded.

"I am the hidden observer," she said.

Every one of us has this hidden observer unconsciously
tracking and remembering and storing the scenes of our life. The
memoirist is always in partnership with that hidden observer,
and the trick of a memoir is to render subconscious observations
in a conscious way.

One of Brenda's favorite students, Mary Matsuda Gruenewald,
struggled for seven years to write her first memoir, *Looking Like the
Enemy: My Story of Imprisonment in Japanese-American Internment
Camps*. She began writing at age seventy-three and published the

memoir at eighty. Mary-san, as the writing class fondly calls this elder, began writing memoir as a legacy for her children.

They kept asking her, "What happened during World War Two when Mama-san, Papa-san, and you were imprisoned in the camps?"

When Mary-san began her memoir, she was a devoted grand-mother and retired nurse who had started the Dial-a-Nurse national hotline. Given her cultural roots, she was also shy and rather stoic. Mary-san was breaking a cultural taboo and generational silence by telling her family's internment camp story. When she first wrote certain scenes—like the FBI invading her farmhouse right after Pearl Harbor—they were clipped, even dissociative. "We burned all of our Japanese treasures before the FBI came," she wrote in one haunting sentence.

The class pleaded with her to expand this harrowing scene. But Mary-san explained that she couldn't really remember that much of the traumatic wartime events. After all, she was only eighteen in 1942. Brenda encouraged Mary-san simply to create "quilt pieces" that the class would all one day help her stitch together.

For years, Mary-san simply wrote scene after scene, trusting that themes and a narrative arc would reveal themselves. They did. And she was amazed at how much detail began to flood into what had at first seemed skimpy memories. Here's an excerpt from the FBI scene, which expanded to four pages in the published book:

That evening after dusk, we brought out the boxes with all of our treasures. The vigorous fire in the oil stove hurled ominous shadows against the white walls of our living room. Papa-san took out all the special Japanese phonograph records and placed them together on one side of the dining room table.

Next to that Mama-san placed all the family pictures from both sides of their families in Japan. Then she brought out all our beautifully crafted Japanese dolls . . .

Slowly I walked to the front of the stove, gave my favorite doll one final squeeze, then flung her into the inferno that seared my heart like some fierce dragon destroying all that I loved. With tears streaming down my face, I turned away but I could still feel the heat and hear the roar of the flames as they consumed her delicate body.

Burning her favorite doll symbolized the tragic losses Mary-san and her family felt. But ironically, with the full telling of this terrible scene and at age eighty, Mary-san began to heal. An exercise Brenda gave her to help her recall and write this traumatic memory was to buy herself a new Japanese doll, place it on her writing desk, and bring it back to life.

"Writing my story not only helped me heal," Mary-san often says. "I'm so happy my story can actually help others, even now." She brought out her second memoir, *Becoming Mama-San*, in 2013. Mary-san is now eighty-nine with enviable energy and passion, and a razor-sharp mind.

HISTORY AND HER-STORY

Of course, Mary-san had the advantage of a chronology that spanned the World War II years, with a beginning and an end and an obvious theme: injustice and its long-term effects. Many of you may also have a natural structure—a Holocaust memoir, a specific time in a country's history, a family event that divides life into a "before and after."

Although not all of us have such a historically dramatic story to tell, *everyone* has a life with turning points, patterns, and discoveries. We all exist in a historical context. Whatever is going on outside us is as important as what is happening inside. So—what time are we in? What setting? What politics? Where are we in the wider world? Whenever you don't know what to write about next, consider these subjects:

- **GENDER**—To one degree or another, it determines your life's story.
- **RACE**—It is often a major factor in how you were raised or treated.
- **POLITICS**—Government and history are the backdrop for your life story.
- **CLASS**—Where you are in the hierarchy of class often shapes your life's plot.
- **CULTURE**—Your culture has helped shape your life in large and small ways.
- **RELIGION**—Belief systems also shape your life story. Track and explore them.
- **LOCATION**—Did you grow up in a city, on a farm, traveling between countries?
- **FOOD**—It is clearly an important element in your childhood and current life.
- **SEX**—Enough said. You can never go wrong exploring sexuality. If nothing else, it moves the plot along!

All of these elements are threads you can follow and weave throughout your memoir. If your memoir doesn't have enough of them, it will lack relevance and certainly not appeal to as wide an audience as you would like. As Lee Gutkind, editor of the magazine *Creative Nonfiction*, writes in *Keep It Real: Everything You Need to Know about Researching and Writing Creative Nonfiction*, "The memoir multiplied creates a million little connections, threading an otherwise fragmented postmodern world with the narrative of human meaning."

SUMMARY VS. STORYTELLING

Many beginning memoirists rely upon a kind of reportorial or summary voice as if they are writing a case history of their own character. They simply describe in expository and dispassionate prose the events of their lives. For example, "My story begins in 1960, when I was eight years old and living in Lansing, Michigan." This is a summary, not a story. It has no voice, no scene, no action, and no dialogue. It's a statement of facts like one would write in a newspaper article. One of Brenda's students actually submitted a memoir piece with bullet points to highlight her life; another offered diary excerpts. While journals and diaries are excellent source material, they need to be fully reimagined and transformed into dramatic scenes for a memoir.

Often we summarize rather than actively narrate our lives because we are reliving difficult times. So we self-censor and protect ourselves from remembered sorrow by detaching from it and writing in a passive voice. One of Brenda's students, Elizabeth Van Deventer, an anthropologist and farmer, wrote a story about nursing her brother, who was dying from AIDS. At first, her writing was almost academic or disembodied, at the very moments it should have been most engaging and raw. Of course, as Elizabeth began to relive those last months with her beloved brother, the process was often very difficult. But as Elizabeth crafted and listened to her classmates' compassionate but rigorous critiques, she began to discover a dark humor, poignant descriptions, vivid dialogue, and a tender interior voice that finally made her story sing. When it was published as "First to Let Go" in the anthology *Secret Histories: Stories of Courage, Risk, and Revelation*, it was an artful and moving elegy of sibling loss and love.

BUILDING AN EPIPHANY

One of the exciting pleasures of any memoir is sharing that moment when the storyteller suddenly understands something for the first time—and then changes the direction of his or her life. These turning-point scenes are the highlights of any life story. Building toward these epiphanies is like tracking an undercurrent to its source. Epiphanies offer a big payoff to both the writer and the reader, but very few people have actually tracked major epiphanies or turning points in their lives. If asked why they moved to New York, they might respond, "A better job" or "To move in with my girlfriend" or "I wanted to be an actor." If you ask someone why they went into their profession, they might have more backstory or buildup to that decision: an influential teacher, a knack for electronics, a seemingly fortunate job offer. If you ask someone why he or she left a marriage, you might get even more explicit details and actual scenes that precipitated the decision: lack of sexual intimacy, an affair, children grown, abuse, or boredom.

Those who have not reflected upon their lives much will often just say, "I suddenly decided to leave . . . [my job, my wife, my home, my country]." This may be enough for casual conversation, but in a memoir it doesn't work to "suddenly" understand something without first carefully constructing scenes that led up to this epiphany.

Crafting epiphanies is like building wings for the reader to soar along with you. Think of each scene in a turning-point chapter as building a section of those necessary wings. At the end, you accept fully how the decision, realization, or epiphany was achieved; then, the reader can also take flight.

FINDING YOUR NARRATIVE ARC

Once Brenda asked a longtime student to bring to class all the "quilt pieces" of her memoir and lay the chapters down on the floor. Over the years of writing, she had decided not to organize her memoir chronologically; she was looking for an overall theme. After a long class discussion, she suddenly recognized the main theme of her life in all the seemingly disconnected chapters. She then knelt on the floor and confidently moved all the chapters into their proper order. It was like watching *The Sorcerer's Apprentice*, where as if animated by magic, every haphazard and disordered thing is set right.

"My life makes perfect sense now," the student murmured, as she sat back on her heels and surveyed all the chapters. "I wouldn't ever have known this if I hadn't written a memoir."

Imagine that building your book is like building a bridge, spanning either a chronological or thematic beginning and end point. Unlike autobiography, which obediently marches along year by year from birth to old age, a memoir may choose just one essential era of your life. A great example of this is artist Marc Chagall's *My Life*. It is what we'd call an "essential" memoir—non-chronological, and focused on the essence of the artist's experience.

Sometimes a memoir will end at the apex of childhood, before the hormonal disarray and drive of adolescence. Other times, the memoir begins and ends with a war or an illness or a divorce. You may write for several years, following chronology, and then you realize your narrative arc is thematic, that your self-discoveries were learned most during a crisis or a relationship or a loss. That time period, then, becomes the bridge of your book, a connection that gives the reader a pathway from meeting the writer to discovering what has shaped your perceptions and choices.

When Brenda was writing *Build Me an Ark: A Life with Animals*, her editor, Jill Bialosky, herself a novelist and memoirist, was very astute. Every time a chapter strayed too far from the theme of animals, Jill wrote in her precise handwriting in the margins: "Off topic" or "Save this" or "How does this family story relate to animals?" and made many cuts. Years later, when Brenda found herself returning to this territory of spirit and animals with *I Want to Be Left Behind*, she had what she thought of as a "bank" of memoir pieces that fit perfectly into the theme of this second memoir.

Nothing is ever really lost in writing a memoir, and so much is found. Your lifetime of writing is like a river that you dam up at certain sections and call that bend in the river a book. But save everything that you think is well written enough to endure, because you never know when it will fit perfectly somewhere else along the flow of your life story. And always keep following that inner thread.

Exercise: Reclaim a Lost Object of Personal History

For Mary Matsuda Gruenewald, reclaiming a favorite Japanese doll as her totem object summed up a powerful life turning point. What is it for you? Remember an important object from your past. Do you know where it is now? Can you find it and set it on your desk and write a story about it? If it is lost, can you find something similar that stirs the same emotions and memories? Follow the feelings and the threads that flow from this found object. It may lead to other objects or memories that become part of your story.

Writing Prompts

The day I lost my favorite _____ was when I knew that _____.

If I had not been overwhelmed by history, I would have _____.

Before I ever understood that _____, I only knew _____.

That turning point in my life marks the beginning of _____.

If I could name one theme of my life, it would be _____.

Everywhere I've traveled, I've always carried _____.

My life is a bridge between _____ and _____.

PUBLISHING TIPS

Agents and editors are always asking authors, "What is your life story's narrative arc?" We've both found that many memoirists have no idea how to shape their story with this forward movement and overarching structure. Many writers are just so happy to get their lives down on the page in some semblance of order that they don't understand that the reader has the same expectations of a memoir that they do of a good novel: a dynamic plot, character development, and captivating scenes.

Often we cannot really know the narrative arc while writing a first draft. But there are things to keep in mind even in the initial stages that will benefit your reader.

1) The plot of any memoir is the evolution of the self through time and events.

2) The main character of a memoir is the narrator (you!), but there are many other players in your life story. Develop *them* fully as characters.

3) Every chapter should have some organizing theme or turning point that adds dramatic and forward movement to the whole book. Just because "it happened" doesn't mean it belongs in your story.

4) Frame each chapter with an underlying theme or thread.

Agents, editors, and readers expect a memoir to be compelling and to build toward some epiphany or resolution, called a "take-away" or even a "payoff." Think of your book as having a narrative architecture. Remember, readers may be looking at your book as a house they can also live in.

3.

YOUR WORLD AS A WRITER

Though you have broken your vows a thousand times, come, yet again, come.

~RUMI

Even when you're not actually writing, you're gathering, witnessing, and engaging with the world as a writer. If you are receptive enough to take it in, *everything is a story*. Though memoir is not a journal, simply recording what goes on day to day, your writing can benefit from regular practice—like meditation. When we meditate, we observe how the mind is always zipping from moment to moment with no beginning, middle, or end. Just the constant skittering of thought, images, and ideas. It's the same with memory, from which the memoir must draw most.

DAILY PRACTICE

When mindfully observing your life, you begin to realize that you can see yourself with less judgment, with more curiosity and compassion. With this expanded awareness, you can discover patterns, perceive connections, and follow threads. These are the building blocks of any good story. The memoirist can observe the flood of memories and ask, "Why this memory now? Is it worth developing? Where does it lead if I follow it to its root?"

Memoirists do more than observe. They organize their memories—sorting and filing them and piecing them together. At first, this assortment is a patchwork collage, but over time, it finds its own form. As you practice, you can discover how to look at even painful stories through the trained eye of a witness. So if you write a story of childhood abuse, the survivor-narrator is witnessing along with the abused child in a compassionate partnership. By revisiting this childhood scene, researchers have discovered that you actually rewire new synapses in your brain to balance the negative experience—and help heal yourself.

If you are willing to observe closely enough, to "sit with" your life stories, even if they are sometimes terrible, you cannot help but establish a profound intimacy with the person you were. You begin to understand what you are so closely observing. As the Zen quote says: "Enlightenment is becoming intimate with everything." Awareness and healing come from this kind of self-study, as well. In memoir, it's not enough just to tell the tale; you must extract some meaning from it for the reader.

For many writers, their work is also a spiritual practice. National Book Award winner Alice Walker says she approaches her work "as if I'm a priestess. I understand that all the forces are being called upon to help me deliver what is most useful and most nourishing for whoever is reading. Even though it's difficult. I also like the idea of encouraging people to grow a bit more fiber in their spirit. Be a bit more strong. Be a bit more adventuresome. Have a bit more courage about encountering what scares you." (For a web link to this interview, see Chapter Notes, page 253.)

READING LIKE A WRITER

How can you write when you don't read? We are always aston Ished when aspiring memoirists tell us that they are *not* reading other memoirs because they "don't want to be influenced" by another's voice or style. That is akin to a dancer saying she doesn't want to study any other choreography except what she makes up herself. How can you learn to write a life story without discovering how others narrate their own stories?

Even though your life is unique, one of the purposes of this book is to show you how we, along with others, have learned to write life stories. When you begin to read a book as a writer, you'll pause midscene and consider "How did she use dialogue to move the plot along?" or "That character just jumps off the page! How did he do that?" or "Wow, I'm flashing around in time but not getting lost. Why not?" Other memoirists can teach you so much, especially if they've successfully resolved these techniques.

Reading is part of your daily practice. It's important to read everything—memoir, fiction, poetry, nonfiction, even magazines and newspapers. When you read a passage you really admire, try to figure out how it was crafted. Imitate it. Study the steps of, say, how an author built toward an epiphany; or how emotional adjectives can brighten prose that is too analytical. Studying how others craft their life stories is the best way you'll learn to write.

WHAT IS THE STORY YOU'RE TELLING TO YOURSELF ABOUT YOURSELF?

One of Brenda's longtime students, John Runyan, came up with this question. It is, we think, one of the most profound mantras for any memoirist. Every day, ask yourself this simple yet provocative question. In the asking, you consider not only who you are on the page, but also what the most important story is about this character who is drawn from you. Some of Brenda's students are so keen on this question that they use it as a writing prompt when they are feeling overwhelmed or lost in the material. It serves as both a lightning rod for your book's main themes and a magnet that attracts all the scattered pieces of your life into some recognizable pattern. Try it yourself. The answers may change as you create your memoir. Pay attention to when and why the answers shift. Follow those signposts as you would a direct GPS signal from your subconscious. Trust those answers. In this way, writing itself is a meditation, a practice that develops you—both heart and soul.

FACING YOUR INNER CRITIC

When you write your life story, you'll reckon with many uncomfortable moments. This process of looking inward at your own shadow is a natural part of the writing process, especially in memoir. Don't be afraid of facing your demons, because conflict, especially what William Faulkner called "the human heart in conflict with itself," is what makes the most compelling story.

Before you attempt an entire memoir, you might start with writing personal essays. They are a more limited and therefore less intimidating canvas: they have a rise and fall of action and introspection, and they often are like clues or even holograms of the larger memoir to come. By working on smaller pieces of your life story, you'll get more confident in building your narrative arc.

One of the best personal essayists and memoirists is Scott Russell Sanders. It took him many years to finally face his father's alcoholism and its devastating effects on his family in his essay "Under the Influence: Paying the Price of My Father's Booze." What is most interesting and healing about this essay is that Sanders looks not only at his father's alcoholism, but also at his own defense against facing the pain—workaholism. By facing his own demons, Sanders concludes that he is still haunted by having learned as a child to "read the weather in faces." His curse and also his cure is writing. "I write, therefore, to drag into the light what eats at me—the fear, the guilt, the shame—so that my own children may be spared."

Not only must you deal with your own shadows, you must also encounter the critics who've taken up residence in your psyche. Whether they spring from internalized parental strictures or cultural taboos or fears, these inner voices can do real damage to the creative process. While the writer takes all the risks, the inner critics stand safely just offstage hurling insinuations:

Who do you think you are?
Who cares about your stupid little life?
Your family will disown you!
You can't tell that story.
You're a liar!

These inner critics are real and dangerous, but they can be called out and held accountable and even put to work. For years, Brenda has taught workshops in "Facing Your Inner Critic." She asks her students to imagine their worst critic, then give him or her a name and a detailed backstory.

For example, one of Brenda's inner critics she named the Drill Instructor. He constantly bullied Brenda and said she was "not serious or literary enough." From morning to dawn, he marched her around with commands: "No book gets written lying down!" or "You're wasting time. Get to work!"

Finally, Brenda decided to write from the Drill Instructor's point of view. She realized this internalized and controlling taskmaster was trying, in his military way, to help Brenda achieve. But the Drill Instructor was so harsh that he often overwhelmed

Brenda and, if not tempered, would drive her into the ground. So Brenda thanked the Drill Instructor for his many skills, but asked him to become a personal assistant so that *she* could give the orders. Dutifully, he followed the new chain of command. The Drill Instructor metamorphosed into an imaginary secretary named Beryl.

For several years, while Brenda was establishing herself as a self-employed writer and teacher, Beryl was a true ally in nudging students to pay tuition on time, in dealing with the demands of publishers, in scheduling and meeting tight deadlines. Beryl actually became quite a protector, and to this day, Brenda can call upon her inner Beryl when she needs toughness, to hold to her writing routine and to stand her ground. Brenda even sends Beryl gifts on National Secretaries Day.

Sarah Jane notes that some of the biggest inner critics she's reckoned with in helping her authors are ones that say:

1) You don't have a good enough story.

2) You don't write easily.

3) Your grammar sucks, and so does your punctuation.

4) You don't have enough time.

5) Fill in the blank with your own fears.

Sarah Jane encourages writers to always answer #5, *Fill in the blank*, because the greatest challenge to writing (or to doing anything for that matter) is fear. As Sarah Jane tells her clients, having courage doesn't mean you aren't afraid. On the contrary, courage means doing whatever it is, despite your fear. As writer Cynthia Ozick says, "If I had to say what writing is, we would have to define it essentially as an act of courage."

What is the story you're telling to yourself about yourself?

Even before you start to write, your story will change you, because it means you have to have courage—to face your fear, to befriend it, to even play with it. But this isn't a one-time deal; confronting your fear once doesn't mean you've conquered it forever. No. Fear is something you might have to face time and time again. And by learning to say "Hello, fear. So what, fear. Get lost, fear," you accomplish two things: you not only change yourself, but you change your readers by sharing your courage with them.

Exercise: The Fifteen-Minute Memoirist

We understand, we truly do, that you are swamped and don't have the time to sit down and write. But can you find fifteen minutes a day? First thing in the morning? At lunch? Early or late evening? Over the period of a year—well, you do the math—that just might be enough time to write your memoir. Everyday exercises in this book are quick ways to trigger your writing, or you can use the prompts in each chapter of this book or other books on the craft of writing. Think of these short spurts of writing as an artist's sketchbook or a photographer's camera, as you open the lens of your inner and outer eyes to tell your true stories.

Exercise: Witnessing Your Life

Try this experiment: Sit quietly and focus your memory on one event from childhood. As this memory unfolds, watch it like a trained observer—a witness—or even a documentary filmmaker. Try to detach from the emotion of the memory and see it more like a film. See how the images flicker in your mind's eye. Now try to stop and fix intently on one image as if it were a still photograph.

Study it and hold it in your mind. Turn it this way and that. Imagine it in another person's scrapbook with that "someone else" explaining it to you from another point of view. Perhaps the person was in that photo with you. What new observations now inform this memory? Is there some vivid detail you see that is different now? Did something hidden suddenly reveal itself?

Write down everything you notice from this exercise. It doesn't have to make sense or fit together—yet. It's all about witnessing your memories with a certain skillful detachment. The practice of writing memoir increases your self-knowledge and your sense of compassion for yourself and others. These skills will enhance your whole life. Brenda, for example, is someone who's learned how to live better through the practice of writing. It has taught her more discipline, structure, and curiosity.

Exercise: Tools of the Trade

You never know when you'll read something, hear some spoken tidbit, or think of an idea—so always keep a notepad and pen, an electronic device, or pocket recorder on hand. New technologies like recording apps on your cell phone or tablet can prompt and assist us as writers more than ever before. Audio or video can enhance your storytelling immensely and bring it to life. So take that video, record that audio idea, snap a photograph that will later inspire you in your writing. Brenda, her students, and other writers are always recommending apps as electronic helpmates, like Voddio for audio/video recording or the many book apps, from Kindle to Kobo to iBooks to Nook.

Then there are those who still like to use pens and notebooks, like Sarah Jane's best-selling author Dick Russell, who carries a reporter's lined notepad and uses shorthand. While working on this book together, Brenda sent Sarah Jane an electronic stylus to use with ZoomNotes, one of the apps that allows you to actually write with a pen on your phone or tablet, and then turn those notes into e-mails or messages. (Not that she uses it. Sarah Jane still prefers a pen and dog-eared notebook.) Some of you remember those handy back-to-school kits that had your favorite No. 2 pencils, binders, crayons, mechanical pencils, and fountain pens? Every writer should make his or her own tools-of-the-trade kit. These will make your daily practice that much easier, more accessible—and even fun.

Writing Prompts

If my life story were a journey, it would be about _____.

My daily practice as a writer is _____.

If I were an omniscient narrator in my own life, I'd realize that _____.

When I witness my own life story, the patterns I see are _____.

I'm going to give my harshest inner critic the name _____. He/she tells me _____.

I can transform my inner critic into an ally by _____.

My favorite tools of the trade are _____.

PUBLISHING TIPS

As a daily practice, anything you do to become more comfortable writing is of great value. While keeping a journal or starting a blog can create a writing routine, if you intend to publish, there's a deep shift—you're no longer writing primarily for yourself. When you write for an audience of any kind, your memoir changes from a private account into a book. It belongs to the wider world. And so do you.

This wide world outside your intimate circle will ask you to do more than become self-aware. Readers want to identify with the "you" who is fully created upon the page. The memoir is like an open door for readers to walk through *and become you*. You are not just an "I" but an eye. You are in a relationship with your reader. And the reader has expectations. It's like the difference between cooking for one and cooking for a dinner party. There are invited guests sitting down to partake of the story you offer them. Be generous.

As a memoirist, you are never really alone but always using your individual experience to connect with the larger world. In an interview with Donna Seaman, a senior editor for *Booklist*, Alice Walker says, "I feel that nothing is truly that personal. If I tell you about some dreadful or joyful thing that has happened to me—if I'm talking to, let us say, 10 people, eight of them will have experienced something similar."

All good books open with a question, which, in one way or another, must be answered by the end of the book. This is the sacred contract an author makes with a reader. And if this contract isn't fulfilled, readers will always feel cheated. Just as an architect does before building a house, or an engineer a bridge, when you become serious about being published, you must methodically construct a plot—beginning with a blueprint, a template—out of the serendipity and chaos of your life. Down the road, you might decide to deviate from it, but it will initially provide the structure you need to get started and keep you focused.

To be published, your creative nonfiction and solid storytelling skills must be honed. It's your truth reconstructed to the best of your recollection. Unless you are running for office or about to be hauled off to jail, readers are not going to question what you did on a Tuesday afternoon fourteen years ago.

An important key to remember if you want to publish is that the author of a good memoir is a guide who takes us on a journey we end up feeling is also our own. As memoirist Kim Barnes writes, "At the end of a memoir, the reader should know more about himself than about the writer."

4.

FIELD NOTES ON YOUR LIFE

The universe is made of stories, not of atoms.
~MURIEL RUKEYSER

Is keeping a journal, a blog, a photo album, or a scrapbook of letters and ideas a good thing? Absolutely! Journaling can be an essential element of your daily writing practice, because it flexes the writing muscles and, like a good massage, loosens the tense ones. Because it is for your eyes only, you are free to express *anything* without worrying about your phrasing, your grammar, your punctuation, or how it all sounds. The process can be wonderfully liberating.

No matter if you jot down notes spontaneously during the day or sit down at a specific time, journal writing can open the door to your subconscious and help bring buried memories to the surface. It is also an effective way of consciously working through dilemmas. In addition to journaling, you may want to keep a record of the little observations, phrases, and thoughts you've experienced or encountered each day. Think of this journal as raw material the way an artist sketches details for later development. Ideally, if you are organized enough, these notes would be kept in a separate notebook that you keep with you wherever you go, or in a folder on your computer or electronic tablet.

Don't worry if you are not journaling daily. It isn't a question of frequency; it's one of doing it when and as you can, and doing it seriously. There's no question that there have been times in Sarah Jane's life when nothing has been as unequivocally helpful. For her, journaling has been a way to look at a painful feeling or an urgent problem, examine it, and then somehow, almost magically, write her way to insight—to a truth that resonates in that moment.

Brenda doesn't do much journaling, nor has she ever kept a diary, except of her dreams. Perhaps her mother's years in the CIA, or the fact that in her family three people had top-security clearance from the US government, instilled in Brenda at a very early age that one's secrets must be hidden or coded. So she kept a rather inscrutable dream journal that no one else could decipher. When she wrote her two memoirs, Brenda turned instead to family photos, letters, Moleskine notebooks, and audio notes that she made with her cell phone recorder app.

These "field notes" to your life are essential to re-create the sensory details and flesh out the epiphanies of any scene. But they are works in progress and not ever ready to be published. Why not? They have not yet been transformed by your conscious craftsmanship into the final creation—your memoir. They are the kneaded clay before the sculpting, glazing, and firing of a beautiful pot. They are life not yet tempered by art.

UNPROCESSED PAIN

Sometimes these journals and field notes are so stream of consciousness, uncensored, and raw that they are what Brenda calls "unprocessed pain." They read like a *cri de coeur*, or "cry from the heart," not like an artfully crafted memoir. One of the best pieces of writing advice Brenda ever received as a young writer was from her first mentor, Diane Johnson. When one of Brenda's dear friends committed suicide in 1981, Brenda wrote about it and sent an early draft to Diane to edit. Very gently, but with her characteristic honesty, Diane advised Brenda to write down every specific detail: the bright spring light in the room when Brenda discovered her friend's body, the freshly folded laundry she was carrying and dropped, the gun gleaming like a dark fist at her friend's cold temple as Brenda felt for a pulse.

"Write down everything you saw and felt that horrible day," Diane gently suggested. "Take notes. Write this story over and over, but don't publish it for several years. Only *then* will you possess and understand it, beyond the trauma. Only then will you discover the larger meaning of this event in your life so you can give it to others."

Gratefully heeding Diane's advice, Brenda wrote down every single thing she could remember at the moment. Then, on the yearly anniversary of her friend's death, Brenda revised the original story. This became a healing ritual, and every draft was more clear-eyed and complete. It took quite a few years until the memoir piece "The Sacredness of Chores," published in *Nature and Other Mothers*, was more than just unprocessed pain, until more than grief framed it. The epiphany of this story was not "surrender to death" but survival. One detail Brenda had scribbled in her notebook about that day was the to-do list she had made before she discovered the suicide. This simple jot in a journal became the theme for the final published story:

TO DO

1) Finish Chapter 10

2) Laundry

3) Defrost fridge

4) Meet P. N. at farmers' market (rhubarb?)

*Always make sure
your reader feels safe.*

At the time of her friend's death, Brenda could never have imagined that this scrawled note would become the organizing principle for a story, the magnet that drew all the seemingly insane pieces together and gave meaning to this loss. A simple to-do list that, at the time, seemed so busy, so foolish, so small set against suicide, would, *upon reflection*, become the sacred death chores of cleaning, of surviving, of staying on. This story ends: "As long as the washer and dryer spin, I tell myself, I am safe and those I love may choose to keep living alongside me. There is laundry to be done and so many chores—chores of living. Think of all the chores we have yet to do, quietly and on our knees—because home is holy."

Whether you're journaling about loss, death, illness, divorce, or any of the painful events that both detour and yet shape our lives, keeping field notes and journals of the raw, unprocessed pain can become the touchstone for your final well-crafted memoir. Writing a memoir can even help heal trauma. As author Amy Greene writes, "It's not forgetting that heals. It's remembering."

KEEPING YOURSELF AND YOUR READERS SAFE

When we do the hard work of understanding the painful events of our own lives, we do not simply pass on the pain. We create something of service to others. We tell stories of the dark side of the moon, the eclipses of our lives—but from the mature memoirist's vantage point of having survived and learned something valuable to others and ourselves.

Many memoirists worry about reengaging with painful periods of their lives. But you really can't expect the reader to feel what you as a writer don't ever want to experience again. There are ways to keep yourself and your readers safe when entering what feels like danger zones or handling emotionally radioactive materials. Remind yourself that these are memories, not your present reality, that you have already survived the blasts, the poisons, and the fears, and are simply here again as if to create a movie scene or set the stage for action over which you now have more control. You are the director, not the actor. You are the storyteller who has many skills and safeguards that you didn't have before. When you summon the courage to revisit a particularly toxic scene, you discover something new or astonishing or healing.

Just as you learn to keep yourself safe as you tell your life story, you also want to make sure your reader feels safe. Do this by signaling that you have survived to tell the tale and know something that will help us. Native American writer and musician Joy Harjo's memoir, *Crazy Brave*, is as harrowing as it is beautiful; but we are given this assurance of her survival in the first pages:

> Though I was reluctant to be born, I was attracted by the music. I had plans. I was entrusted with carrying voices, songs, and stories to grow and release into the world, to be of assistance and inspiration . . . It is this way for everyone . . . we each have our own individual soul story to tend.

Harjo's memoir was years in the writing, and her prose moves like poetic jazz with surprising key changes. Her life story is told with a tender authenticity that comes from singing the story of a hard-lived life. No matter the mandatory boarding school, the tragic family history, and the abusive, alcoholic Pueblo poet ex-husband, Harjo shows in every scene that she is a true survivor.

That's why we can continue reading and living her story alongside her. "I followed poetry," she writes in *Crazy Brave*. "I let my thought of forgiveness for myself and for others in the story follow the waves of the ocean in prayer."

Like Joy Harjo, when you tell your life story, you also teach others how to survive, how to forgive, how to interpret and find value in the past. Readers can stand on your shoulders to see their way a little farther—because you've gone before us. You never know what astonishing events people have survived until they tell their stories.

DREAMS AND LETTERS

For the writer, dreams are a major step in the alchemy of turning lead into gold. Dreams are fertile and symbolic transliterations of reality. Sometimes they let us glimpse our "real" life with a wit and detachment and wisdom that our waking selves lack.

In the anthology *Writers Dreaming: Twenty-Six Writers Talk about Their Dreams and the Creative Process*, Naomi Epel turned her day job into a book. While hosting the radio show *Dreamtalk*, Epel also worked as a literary escort; she often shepherded sleepless and exhausted authors around on book tours when they visited San Francisco. Starting with the simple question "Have you ever had a dream that influenced your work?" Epel interviewed writers as diverse as Isabel Allende, Elmore Leonard, and Anne Rice. Though most of the authors in her collection are novelists, their recurring nightmares, precognitive dreams, and themes are like memoir—stories drawn from their real lives and imaginations.

In *Writers Dreaming*, author Maya Angelou reveals that when she has a certain recurring dream of climbing a tall building like the Arc de Triomphe, she knows that her writing is going well. Angelou credits her dreams for helping her work out writing problems. "One sees that the brain allows the dreamer to be more bold than he or she ever would be in real time," she says. Angelou also refers to a West African phrase, "deep talk," meaning that you never really find the answer but you can continue to dive deeper into the questions. "Dreams may be deep talk," she concludes.

Another place a memoirist might find "deep talk" is in letters. Sometimes when we are not thinking about craft or finding the perfect technique or style, we actually tell our life stories more completely. Many writing teachers use the exercise of writing letters to your younger self. But for those of us who have actually collected letters or journals from our younger years, these can be a treasure trove of prompts and reminders of who we once were and the way we used to see the world. A perfect example of this is Richard Hugo's poetry collection *31 Letters and 13 Dreams*, based on his old letters and dreams.

In your memoir, think of the voice you use when you open your heart to your best friend, revealing deep, dark truths while, perhaps unconsciously, working at keeping them (and possibly yourself) interested, even amused. Be your own Scheherazade. Sometimes the voice of your letters is more engaging and accessible than the written voice of your actual memoir. Several of Brenda's students were fortunate or foresighted enough to have saved volumes of their letters and journals since childhood. They have a real head start on making a memoir with this rich record of personal history at their fingertips. Since Brenda moved so often during her early years, she had very few written records of her childhood. But as luck would have it, several of her friends from college and her early years actually saved all of Brenda's letters and sent them to her when they heard she was writing a memoir. These are invaluable personal histories—and excellent for fact-checking. These days many people are practically living online with Facebook, Twitter, Instagram, and e-mail. You can store this abundance of raw material "in the cloud," but be sure to keep backup files on flash drives or external hard drives. These will be part of the priceless, and sometimes secret, archives that you revisit as you create your life story.

AGELESS

As you excavate the many layers of personal history in your field notes, dreams, letters, and journals, you may begin to see revealing patterns and connections. There is often an unexpected and quite wonderful side effect: you feel almost a mystical sense of timelessness. You understand what Albert Einstein meant when he said that time is simply a construct, not a real limit. Matching physics, there are some philosophies, especially in the East, that teach us to simply see this life as connected to many past and future lives. In a way, a memoir constructs a life story as if it were a series of past lives folded into this current one.

When Sarah Jane and Brenda give "Life Story" workshops, some of the participants are initially anxious. There are two groups of writers who tend to be more intensely worried than the rest—the youngest and the oldest. The youngest, because they feel they haven't lived long enough to have a story to tell, and the oldest, for almost the same reason, but reversed. Their concern is—who cares about their past? Both the very young and the very old are making the same mistake. They believe that it's the sum total of their life experiences that matters. It might seem counterintuitive to say that's not what matters. What actually matters is what story you choose to tell and the depth, not the width or span, of your experience.

Gertrude Stein wrote, "We are always the same age inside." The more you delve into your own life, tracking your growth and self-discovery, the more you experience a sense of existing both in and out of a specific time. This is because you are working on different stages of self and are therefore not stuck in the present or past. You are ageless, and gone are those inner critics who whisper, "You're too old [or too young] to write a memoir."

There are stunning examples of memoirs written by authors in their nineties, as well as by teenagers. Too bad infants can't write. As an agent, Sarah Jane would love to have the memoir of a newborn, about her nine-month journey in the womb and then out into the light. We don't have newborns, but we do have Anne Frank, who was only thirteen when she first went into hiding and started writing her harrowing and yet beloved *Diary of a Young Girl*. Then there is *Girl, Interrupted*, by Susanna Kaysen, which tracks the attempted suicide and incarceration of an eighteen-year-old girl in a psychiatric hospital—a self-admitted visit that was supposed to last for weeks and went on for two years.

On the other end of the spectrum is Captain James Arruda Henry. He published his autobiography, *In a Fisherman's Language*, when he was ninety-eight. But what is most remarkable about his story is that he was illiterate for most of his life and didn't even learn to read and write until he was ninety-one. Harry Bernstein also comes to mind. After years of seeing his manuscripts rejected, he finally became a published author at the age of ninety-six, with his first memoir, *The Invisible Wall: A Love Story That Broke Barriers*. His two following memoirs, *The Dream* and *The Golden Willow: The Story of a Lifetime of Love*, have been compared to Frank McCourt's *Angela's Ashes* and the writing of Isaac Bashevis Singer.

All of these memoirs are signs that whether you're very old or very young, or somewhere in between, there is, as librarian, author, and critic Nancy Pearl says, "an insatiable curiosity about other people's lives."

IS GENDER THE SAME AS VOICE?

As it is for age, so it is for gender: whether you're a woman or a man obviously makes a difference in your life experiences and perspectives. But in the long run, only story and voice matter. Voice often comes more quickly and naturally to women. Women are used to having "BFFs" and whispering the intimate details and secrets of their hearts to them. That personal voice is also available to men, but it may be harder to access, because they have fewer outlets for it and less permission to explore aspects of their inner lives. In fact, many little boys possess that sensitivity, but society and culture slowly drum it out of them and they then have to work their way back to it.

When Sarah Jane's daughter, Elisabeth, was seven, she had a best friend, a little boy we'll call David. Elisabeth was, as she still is, very much a girlie girl but she was also (and continues to be) outspoken, matter-of-fact, and spunky. While she was kind-hearted, she could also be surprisingly sharp-tongued. David, on the other hand, was incredibly sensitive and gentle. He was a dear little boy who tended to get easily upset. David's family would have preferred that he be more rough-and-tumble like his younger brother.

One day, as Sarah Jane was walking Elisabeth and David home from school for a play date, a screaming and filthy woman approached. She was dressed in rags and had a cigarette hanging from her lips. Every so often, she would cough outrageously. Sarah Jane tried to shield the children, but to no avail. David was clearly devastated by the sight of this woman, whereas Elisabeth sized up the situation, calmly took David's hand and said, "You see, David, that's what happens when you smoke."

Elisabeth realized in those early school years that it was perfectly okay for a girl to be both feminine and tough—to be interested in lipstick and high heels, but also to play a mean game of

volleyball. For boys, on the other hand, it was mostly unaccept-
able to be sweet and sensitive, to want to cuddle and be reassured.
Some men, even though they got toughened up, managed never to
fully abandon their connection to that tenderness. It is those men,
like Frank McCourt, or Tobias Wolff, who wrote *This Boy's Life*,
whose memoirs we fall in love with.

PUBLISHING TIPS

Sarah Jane as agent and Brenda as writing teacher have come upon
"complete manuscripts" that are simply transcribed journals.
Please remember this: if you want to publish, your journal is *not*
your memoir. Your journal is the grist, the fodder, the seeds; it is
not the baked, ready-to-eat bread. Your journal, no matter how
revealing or how startling, is part of your private experimentation
lab, not ever the finished product. Fully baked, ready-to-eat bread
is neither a series of disconnected episodes nor an accounting of
"how I worked it out." It is a story, or a series of them, with a narrative arc: a beginning, a middle, and an end.

It would be disingenuous of us to suggest that ageism doesn't
exist. Sarah Jane herself admits she is leery when she receives a
letter saying things like: "I'm seventy and have finally decided
to write my memoir" or "Although I'm only fifteen, I write really
well and my parents say this is truly amazing!" Tell an agent or
editor about your story, not about your age. If your story has an
original voice or content, if it captures the imagination, no agent
will care about how young or old you are, or whether you're a
woman or a man.

These days, you should send your query to an agent by e-mail.
Don't say that you're too old or too young to have an e-mail
account or to know what a Word document is. If you don't have
an e-mail account of your own, use a friend's, your parents', or

your children's. And if the concept of a Word document is alien to you, ask someone to explain it. While it's not necessary to have a cell phone, you do have to provide a telephone number where you can be easily reached and where one can leave messages.

It is also important, especially if you are telling a story about something that happened in the past, to clue the reader in to what is happening to you now, in the present. For example, Rena Kornreich Gelissen, who was born in Poland in 1920, begins her searing memoir, *Rena's Promise: A Story of Sisters in Auschwitz*, with a story of how an American Jewish doctor in 1994, a year before her book was published in the United States, offered to remove the tattooed number from her arm. In that short prologue, we learn a lot about Rena's present life.

Recently, a friend asked Sarah Jane to read the memoir of her longtime boyfriend, who was turning eighty. He had decided to write his life story for his grandchildren. While the writing was fine, what was missing was context. By context we mean acknowledging your audience, telling them what was happening in the world when you were born, and, finally, letting them know what your life is like now. Without that, it is hard to situate your story in time, so the reader is left in limbo.

Does age matter? Does gender make a difference? Of course they do. Your story changes, depending on your perspective. It changes if you are telling the story of a woman or a man, and it's different if your memoir is written from the point of view of someone who is looking back on events, or someone who is just starting out. Ultimately, however, regardless of your age or gender, what matters is your ability to transmit to your reader the relevance and immediacy of your story, to convey the nuance and depth of your understanding. Do so, if possible, with a touch of authenticity and wit. Come to think of it, maybe it is not a baby, but a centenarian who will write about the journey into and out of the womb.

Exercises: Pieces of Your Past

Ask your family, friends, and acquaintances if they will send you copies of your letters from younger years.

Begin to keep a dream journal as well as a daily or waking-life notebook.

Look at one of your letters side by side with a page from your memoir. Is your letter livelier, more engaging, or more truthful? If so, try to re-create that style in your memoir.

Create a scrapbook specifically for your memoir. Include letters, journal excerpts, photos, and dreams. Sometimes just opening this scrapbook is enough to trigger memories that you once thought lost.

Find material objects, treasures, or other possessions from your past that summon, in genie fashion, memories. Write a scene based on each of these objects. Their stories will engage and surprise you.

Exercise: Proprioceptive Writing

At the beginning of every "Life Story" workshop, Sarah Jane always introduces writers to a method with the odd name of "Proprioceptive Writing." If daily journaling is like exercise, PW, as its advocates and originators have dubbed it, is like meditating, doing yoga, tai chi, or qigong on paper. And yes, it *does* involve paper. Writing with paper and pen engages the mind and body. It awakens a primal genetic connection between your hand and your brain in a way that typing on a keyboard and looking at a screen often can't.

The full description of the PW technique is available in a book called *Writing the Mind Alive: The Proprioceptive Method for Finding Your Authentic Voice* by Linda Trichter Metcalf, PhD, and Tobin Simon, PhD.

Sarah Jane, who is the agent for the book and had the benefit of taking workshops and instruction from Linda, feels that these teachings are uniquely precious.

Here is a brief description of the PW method:

Start with several sheets of unlined white paper and a favorite pen. A "Write," which is what a twenty- to twenty-five-minute Proprioceptive Writing exercise is called, is done to music, specifically baroque music, such as Bach, Handel, Pachelbel, or Vivaldi (the slower movements work best), so you will need to have access to the appropriate CDs or digital files. If you don't like baroque music, try classical Indian or Japanese Zen music; Sarah Jane has found that they can evoke a similar response. Linda and Tobin suggest that you also light a candle, to give the sense of creating a sacred space.

In PW there are three rules:

1) Write what you hear.

Treat your thoughts as spoken words, and write them down exactly as you hear them in the moment, as if you are a scribe overhearing your thoughts. Linda and Toby say, "Slooow down and turn up your hearing."

2) Listen to what you write.

Arguably, hearing is the most actively engaged sense, and listening is the skill that you need to practice most. Linda and Toby say that a Write isn't a writing skill at all, that it's a hearing skill. "It's hearing yourself," they say.

3) Be ready to ask the proprioceptive question.

Which is simply: "What do I mean by _____?" Into that blank insert a written word, phrase, or expression that has caught your attention. Be ready to ask this question of yourself at any moment. Don't worry about interrupting the Write. Asking the question is how you reach that deeper truth. Remember, this is not about writing—it's about feeling, thinking, understanding, and getting to a truth.

In a Write, always write out the full question and also, of course, the answer you hear in response. Take nothing for granted.

Writing Prompts

If I hadn't lived through the tumultuous sixties in America, I would never have known_____. [Substitute any time and place.]

Because I kept all my letters from that time, I realized that
_____.

My letters home from [the war, college, camp] tell a very different story than I ever tell my friends. In them, I only reveal _____.

It was a dream that first foretold _____.

Once, in a notebook, my younger self decided, wrongheadedly, to
_____.

5.
SHOWING UP: CREATING A CHARACTER OF THE SELF

The opposite of self-consciousness is generosity.

~BRENDA UELAND, *IF YOU WANT TO WRITE: A BOOK ABOUT ART, INDEPENDENCE AND SPIRIT*

Know thyself—the wisdom of the ancient Delphic oracle—was carved into the stone temple of the Greek god Apollo. This guiding principle might also be the maxim for any memoirist. Self-discovery, a larger understanding of oneself and the world, are the offerings of a good memoir, both for the writer and the reader. When we read a life story, we expect the writer to take us on a journey of what the Greeks called *gnosis*, or knowledge. In a memoir, this means *self-knowledge*. As we will say often in this book, the plot and movement of any successful memoir is the evolution of the self. If you don't grow and change in the telling of your life, the reader will not receive your hard-earned wisdom. It's what editors and agents call "the payoff." We call it good storytelling.

Readers experience the memoirist's life as if it is happening to them—and the writer is simply a doorway into the compelling story. Imagining yourself as a vehicle for the story, instead of the star, also gives you a little space from feeling too naked or exposed. Although it sounds like a contradiction, after some time, you will finally and fully realize that *you* are the main character of a memoir.

If you don't understand yourself more at the end of your memoir than you did at the beginning, if you are stuck in the same old patterns, if you haven't found some clarity and detachment from your foibles, then the memoir has no forward motion—it's static. It's what Sarah Jane calls, a "misery memoir." It repeats the same conflicts over and over again, without any resolution. Jean-Paul Sartre wrote an entire play about people trapped in their own patterns and their lack of self-knowledge. It was called *No Exit*. And that's how the reader feels if you don't actively grow and change in your life story.

SIDESTEP THE SELF

In memoir, it is usually the first person, or "I" who narrates the story. In the same way an actor will create a character for the stage, you can craft a character of yourself on the page. But remember that you as the writer are slightly detached and distinct from the "I" on the page. That person is not exactly you, with all of your secrets exposed, but someone who is a carefully reconstructed replica of yourself. In fact, this creation is another creature altogether—a sympathetic and fully realized companion, an artfully portrayed character who is you, but not all of you.

In creating this character on the page, you can still keep something hidden, something not vital to the story, something too personal or not too relevant. You are safe then, because you have control over what you choose to reveal. Ironically, this technique of sidestepping the self, allows you to confide more, to be more revealing and trusting of the reader. Only when the writer makes the decision to hold some details of her life in reserve, to keep them private, is she able to create a full portrait of herself as a character.

For example, while some memoirists make their love lives center stage, others choose to keep their personal romances private, especially if they are not the focus or theme of the memoir. Students are always asking, "Do I have to tell *that* story?" The answer is, only if that detail is relevant to your character's evolution. For example, if a marriage, abortion, or unknowingly fathering a child is a defining moment in your life and shapes your character, then it should be included. If it distracts from the character development and doesn't serve the theme or plot of the book, then there is no need to tell the reader. The art of selection—what goes in and what stays out—is one of the most vital, and yet often bewildering, decisions you'll make about your memoir.

One way to visualize selecting what parts of your character belong on the page is to actually draw a timeline of your life so far. Get a long strip of paper and tack it up on a wall. Jot down the major events of your life on a chronological series of sticky notes. Be sure to include dates, settings, and some historical context of the world around you. Then stand back from your timeline. Scan it deeply to discover your turning points, which of those events most shaped your character, your life decisions, and who you would become. Those events that do not support the major themes or character development of your life story, simply remove from your visual timeline. As you make these editorial decisions, always remember that character evolution is the narrative arc and plot of any memoir.

Sidestepping and reflecting upon the self to carefully re-create that person on the page is one of the most liberating things we can teach you. There are some wonderful techniques to help you understand this vital commute between younger and older selves. For example, one of Brenda's students, a remarkable psychotherapist, Dianne Grob, was writing about a time in her early life when she was struggling with her own severe depression. Grob writes in her memoir, *What the Heart Wants: Stories of Hope and Belonging*, "I was thirty-nine years old and for three decades, I had lived inside despair: aware of my own vulnerability and the vulnerability of everything I held dear." If she were not writing with the grace and generosity of a mature narrator, Grob might have stayed on that somber note of sorrow throughout her entire memoir. But her next thought signals to the reader that she is offering us something remarkable and essential to us all: "I did not yet know how to love the world . . ." Her mature narrator tells us this poignant truth about her younger self, then implies that she will learn to "choose hope."

When you say, *This is what I knew then, but this is what I know now*, your mature narrator reassures the reader that the author is not so enmeshed with the character that there is no self-knowledge. Brenda sent a final draft of her memoir *I Want to Be Left Behind* to one of her longtime editors, Maureen Michelson, who is the publisher and editor in chief of NewSage Press. "I love the humor in

---

The plot and movement of any successful memoir is the evolution of the self.

---

your book," Maureen said. "But *now* you need to turn that same irreverent and witty lens you use for other characters upon your-self. Try not to see yourself as just a misfit, misunderstood by your family—but rather as a rebel who defied and questioned their deep-seated beliefs."

This was the last criticism Brenda wanted to hear, especially with a book that had a deadline looming. But Maureen reminded her: "After all, it's only fair that you show the reader how foolish, wrongheaded, and even sometimes fundamentalist, you might look to others." This editorial critique was so perceptive that Brenda went back through the book and wove in many more scenes that revealed more foibles and flaws of her own character.

Here's one passage from a scene in which Brenda's mother comes up from Georgia to visit her daughter; she insists that they attend the only Southern Baptist church they can find in Manhattan. It is in Harlem, and they are the only white faces in the congrega-tion. City-wise Brenda is convinced they will be mugged. She frets that her mother, who is wearing a polyester flower-print dress and go-to-church hat, and carrying a fuchsia handbag, might as well be wearing a sandwich board proclaiming, "Mug Me! I'm from Out of Town!" But as her mother chats it up with the deacon, heart-ily sings gospel, and socially sips chicory coffee with the other church ladies, Brenda realizes: "My mother, a Southern Baptist conservative, had fewer racial stereotypes here in Harlem than her liberal daughter who carried mace in her purse and was hyper vigilant on city streets. Mother had entered this church with a much more open heart than mine." (See Chapter Notes, page 253, for a web link to Brenda's *Book Lust* interview with Nancy Pearl.)

When you reveal in a memoir your own character's faults and quirks, the reader trusts you more. This also creates an alliance between the author and the reader that the character will figure things out, will finally "get it" and change. This alliance is really key to bonding with your reader. It's as if reader and author are empathetically united in rooting for the self to become not perfect, but more fully conscious.

THIRD-PERSON AND FIRST-PERSON OMNISCIENT

When a writing student is having trouble imagining how he might appear to others, Brenda will ask him to switch from first to third person. When referring to the "I" as "she" or "he," there is a sudden opening to another point of view, another reality. Third person also allows a certain calm detachment, especially when recalling painful scenes—just a little space to consider what was learned from that difficult time.

A *New York Times* article, "This Is Your Life (and How You Tell It)," notes that in therapeutic situations, when people were narrating traumatic scenes from their lives, "the third-person perspective allowed people to reflect on the meaning of their social miscues . . . and thus to perceive more psychological growth." Switching from first-person to third-person omniscient allows the storyteller to see *all sides* of a story. And there is another benefit, as the article concludes: "Mental resilience relies in part on exactly this kind of autobiographical storytelling, moment to moment, when navigating life's stings and sorrows." (See Chapter Notes, page 253, for a web link to this article.)

This exercise of switching points of view helped Brenda when she was creating a self-portrait of herself as a child. In the third-person omniscient point of view she made a discovery that she then could switch back into first person. Here is that epiphany: "I didn't realize that I was an odd, rather wild, and unknowingly subversive child."

Brenda also teaches a strategy of self that she calls "first-person omniscient." It is perhaps the most difficult point of view for a memoirist, but it is often the most clear-eyed. An example of first-person omniscient is in James Carroll's *An American Requiem*, in which the novelist-turned-memoirist describes a 1960 photo of his adolescent self with his family when they were granted an audience with the pope. Using his novelistic skills, Carroll describes Pope John XXIII's audience with his devout family. But regarding himself, Carroll writes:

> This lad—how in seeing him in this photo now, I would love to embrace him, pressing in all that I have seen and learned of acceptance and forgiveness and affirmation. He is my younger self, of course, and there is nothing I can do for him.

While first-person omniscient is rare and really hard to achieve, this passage shows how rewarding it is for the reader. (See Chapter Notes, page 253, for a web link to an excerpt from *American Requiem*.)

THE MATURE NARRATOR AND THE YOUNGER SELF

The memoirist who narrates with the full range of his or her being can become what Brenda calls "the mature narrator." Ideally, this mature narrator has spent years witnessing the younger self, without judgment or blame. The mature narrator has access to all selves—child, adolescent, adult, and elder. The reader trusts a narrator who can skillfully navigate this latitude and longitude of a life story. When the mature narrator is telling your story, the reader receives the gifts of your hard-earned wisdom. It's one of the reasons we read memoir. We want to learn what *you've* learned about life.

The mature narrator is not always the easiest voice to discover, especially if you are telling stories that are painful, or, if you're still struggling with any narrative post-traumatic stress, such as a death, a battle, or an accident.

When Brenda was working at the *New Yorker*, her boss and coworker came running into the office one day. Mrs. Walden was flushed and distraught, already reaching for her cigarettes with a shaky hand. Grace, a young writer, strode in, her face ashen but her demeanor calm and determined. She was already jotting in her ever-present Moleskine notebook. Here's how Brenda tells the story:

"Oh my God," Mrs. Walden shrieked. "It was horrible, just *horrible!*" Then she shook her head and crashed down in her chair.

"What?" we all demanded.

"I can't believe I'm still alive . . . so close. It could have been me!"

"What happened? What's going on?" we all chimed in, frustrated by the lack of detail. We had no idea if the horror was outside, inside, or imminent. Were we in danger, too?

"You think you're going to live forever," Mrs. Walden continued, almost under breath. We had to lean near to hear her. "Then, in a flash, you get hit by a car and you're dead!" She burst out weeping, dropping her cigarette on the floor. Someone had to fetch it and snuff it out so it wouldn't burn down the entire building.

Now alarmed and worried, everyone turned to Grace in the hope of finally finding out what had happened. Grace scribbled a few more notes and then, with a deep intake of breath, she closed her Moleskine. Grace composed herself, perched on a desk, and began in an unruffled voice.

"Mrs. Walden and I were standing on the street corner at Forty-Second Street. Suddenly a yellow cab lost control, careened through the pedestrians in the walkway, and plowed into the bank window. Glass shattered, people scattered. The car didn't stop until it struck the tellers' counter, knocking people down, kind of like wooden soldiers." Grace paused to reflect and then added, "I think some people must have died, but I couldn't see through the crowds. It was . . . terrible."

"And I barely escaped!" Mrs. Walden again found her voice.

But nobody was listening to her. We didn't trust her to tell the story. Her narrator was all reaction, with no discernible action. Mrs. Walden's fear was so intrusive that we couldn't even see any of the other characters or the story.

Grace was the mature narrator, while Mrs. Walden dissolved into an unreliable narrator, so overcome with the drama and her own emotional response that she literally couldn't see straight. One technique Grace might have used to tell this accident years later was to begin it: "I did not know that a lunchtime stroll would change the way I saw the city and convince me I was no longer safe even just walking on a sidewalk. Soon after, I would leave Manhattan." The mature narrator can frame a scene at the beginning, in the middle, or at the end—by stepping in for a sentence or two at a very high point of action, like an accident, and reflecting upon its influence on her life.

Think of your mature narrator as a very steady handheld camera witnessing a difficult, dramatic scene. That camera doesn't veer chaotically around a room or fuzz out or drop the viewer during the action. The camera is centered, focused, not only *in* the story but also observing and dependably keeping its lens open and stable—so we can clearly see what's going on. And always carry your notebook. You never know when a story is going to come to you.

COMPASS OF CHARACTERS

Think of all the people in your memoir, including yourself, as navigating around a compass of characters. Just as we can travel the world using a magnetic compass, so we also journey through our life story being moved and motivated by others. You as the narrator are not automatically the true north of your memoir's compass. We define that true north as the catalyst or trigger of all the action.

In early drafts, you may not be able to identify your true north or south, but over time, you can assess the person who most influences everyone else, including yourself. For Barack Obama, in *Dreams from My Father*, true north is his search for the Kenyan man who gave him life but who he barely knew. In an interesting example of how two siblings might tell their shared childhood from very different and sometimes conflicting points of view, we have Geoffrey and Tobias Wolff. One parent is the catalyst for each brother's memoir. The older brother, Geoffrey, wrote *The Duke of Deception: Memories of My Father* with a razor-sharp focus on his fascinating but flimflam father, who sets the whole family in motion with his chaotic and yet compelling schemes. Younger brother, Tobias, in *This Boy's Life*, focuses on their mother—and the two memoirs read as if the boys were raised in two different realities. In fact, the brothers were separated by distance and time. Tobias is much the younger, and when the parents divorced, they also divided their children. Tobias went west with his mother, and Geoffrey stayed on the East Coast with his con-artist father. Though both authors write about both parents, a different parent serves as true north for each memoir. (See Chapter Notes, page 253, for a web link to an article on the Wolff brothers.)

Often the true south character is the memoirist, who, in opposition or reaction to the true north character, is challenged, nourished, outraged, inspired, or simply bewildered. Around that compass circle, you can also determine the west and east characters. Then set the compass of characters spinning and follow the drama. One note here: Sometimes true north may not be a person but a country, a religion, an event—like a war or a famine or 9/11.

Sometimes it is one haunting scene that, like true north, keeps you magnetized as you navigate the story of your life.

CREATING AN ANTAGONIST

How many of us are often more drawn to a story's villain than to the hero? A memoir with a first-person narrator can run the risk of being so one-sided, so much the memoirist's sense of what's right and wrong, that the reader chafes at being trapped in one person's moral universe. The enduring characters in novels or memoirs are much more nuanced, conflicted, always struggling with their own shadows. Think of Shakespeare's antihero Hamlet or the tragic flaws of Oedipus. In those gray areas, there is so much room for growth and movement. But in black-and-white characters, the plot is simply about one's own goodness prevailing over or losing out to the dark.

What if other characters who may seem like antagonists to your protagonist are actually more interesting? Beware of the tendency to portray yourself so self-righteously that you become a tin Jesus shining among stereotypical villains. The more well-drawn the villain or antagonist, the more we root for the hero or self. This is because the struggle between our own bright potential and our inner demons is a universal and timeless plot. Creating a worthy opponent in that struggle is more truthful than making paper tigers of our antagonists. To create well-drawn antagonists, we must give them their time onstage and admit our own flaws. This requires a lot of stretching on our part to allow others their story in the midst of our own.

Our favorite definition of *intelligence* is "the ability to tolerate a high degree of ambiguity." This, of course, includes a sense of ambiguity about your own character, and understanding that there may be more layers of meaning and points of view than your own. When you write a memoir, you'll become more comfortable with your own flaws, including gaps in your memory. It is ironic, but when you question your memory and reveal self-doubts and flaws, the reader actually trusts you more.

ONE SCENE THAT EXPLAINS YOUR WHOLE LIFE

Like any good storyteller, you can learn how to set scenes and how to craft active dialogue, along with strong description, interior, and plot. Imagine a stage or movie. Now imagine that you are allowed only one scene that explains your whole life. Like a hologram, let this one scene shimmer in your mind. It should contain the major themes and emotions of your larger story. The listener or reader can glimpse the greater whole in this one scene. The first time you do this one-scene exercise, set it in childhood, when your senses were new and alive.

Memoirist Maxine Hong Kingston reveals a literal mother lode of material in her famous memoir, *The Woman Warrior*. The book begins with one of the most original and haunting opening lines of any memoir:

"You must not tell anyone," my mother said, "what I am about to tell you."

Then Kingston hears the terrible truth about her aunt's death in China. All action is triggered at this moment of secret sharing. This family secret will haunt and define Kingston's story. It is one scene that explains Kingston's whole life; it is her true north.

Your "one scene" should give the reader not just a vivid picture but also an emotional charge. A successful life story reads more like narrative "true fiction." It employs all the techniques of a good novel. Most of all, an engaging memoir is carefully constructed and built scene by scene. These scenes have a "burden of proof" to achieve that requires more than the simple telling.

EACH SCENE HAS THREE JOBS TO DO

Just recreating the details and action of a scene isn't enough. Description, setting, dialogue, and interior are only parts of it. Each scene should achieve more than one thing. Study each of your scenes and ask these questions:

Does this scene advance the plot?
Does it deepen the characterization?
Does this scene engage your major themes?

To reveal your life and self-portrait on the page takes time and technique. Like the quickening of pregnancy, the reader can feel when the memoirist suddenly comes alive on the page.

PUBLISHING TIPS

When Sarah Jane compared notes with her associate Jessica Sinsheimer, they both admitted to being prejudiced against any story that begins with the cliché of a character waking up from a dream as the alarm clock goes off, or a description of the weather—you know, the "dark and stormy night" syndrome. Of course, there are exceptions: waking up to the devastating storm Katrina approaching a Louisiana bayou; or Hurricane Sandy bearing down on New Jersey beaches; or the 2004 tsunami in the Indian Ocean that killed more than two hundred thirty thousand people in fourteen countries. But short of such dramatic events, be cautious about beginning a story with your alarm clock or the weather—be it stormy, steamy, or frigid. Start with a scene that is unique to your book.

Just as you create a character of yourself, do the same with everything in your memoir—the animate as well as the inanimate; all must have unique personalities. Sarah Jane also says that your memoir will be richer and more interesting when you allow the other people in your life to make significant appearances and, you allow *them* to shine. In the memoir *The Glass Castle*, even though Jeannette Walls is the author and main character, it's often her deeply flawed but charismatic mother, Rose Mary Walls, that we most remember.

Although you are likely the main character in your memoir, populate it with other vulnerable and petty, sometimes wonderfully generous, and often annoyingly or endearingly quirky people (and other creatures). The reader will feel greater warmth and kinship toward you if you aren't always the main player or the hero.

One of the ways to ensure that you have other angles of vision when creating yourself on the page is to have several fully engaged and critical readers along the way. We always suggest that a memoirist find a good writing class at a university or community college. Or you can join a writer's critique group and settle in to learn the craft of memoir and how to tell an original life story.

Your memoir is neither an autobiography nor a confessional in which you write about everything you've ever done, known, and felt. Rather, it is an edited version of your life. A memoir that you write to be published, although it might invite readers to share certain events of your life must also—like a good mystery—engage and captivate them. Sarah Jane always tells her clients to approach their memoir as though they were writing a novel—a novel that just happens to be (mostly) true.

Exercise: First-Person Sketches

One of Brenda's favorite exercises for memoirists is to write four one-page first-person sketches, each from a different point of view. Write a portrait of your character (your "self") from the point of view of:

1) Someone who loves you

2) Someone who will never understand you

3) Someone who despises you

4) Someone who wants very much to understand you

Exercise: Creating a Compass of Characters

Draw a circle, and pinpoint which character is the true north, true south, east, and west. Navigate this circle, and watch how the magnetic attractions and repulsions play a part in your story. Keep in mind that this compass may change as your writing progresses. A productive exercise Brenda gives her students is to create a one-sentence description that sums up the core of another character. Then support this perception with an active scene:

He was a man who _____. (Example: "He was a man who would admit no peers.")

She was a woman who _____. (Example: "She was a woman who heard everything—even when it was not spoken.")

Exercise: Visual Storyboards

Finding visuals or show-and-tells to help illustrate your life is a good working tool. Family photos are a wonderful way to jump-start your memories and your storytelling. Photo images let us practice the art of reflection and observation from a more detached perspective. They are like flash cards for memoirists. Play with them. Arrange them in different orders, not just chronologically. See if there are emerging patterns. Can you make a kind of visual storyboard of your family photos?

Now, choose only one photo and tell its story. Try writing this story in first-person, and then again in third-person omniscient. See how different the story of this one photo becomes when you use another point of view besides first person.

On your storytelling shrine, place this one photograph.

Writing Prompts

What I did not know then about myself was _____.

Looking back, I understand _____.

When I was a child, I didn't realize that _____.

It would take me years to know that _____.

I did not realize that I was a rather _____, _____, and _____ child.

6.
WHERE AM I?:
A SENSE OF PLACE
AND TIME

We did not come into this world. We came out of it, like
buds out of branches and butterflies out of cocoons.

~LYALL WATSON, *GIFTS OF UNKNOWN THINGS*

Just as important as the question "Who am I?" is "Where am I?"
Setting is a memoir's main stage, and it needs detailed designing,
historical context, and fascinating backdrops to prop up all the
drama. Novelists know that a sense of place and time is critical to
the story. But many memoirists often forget that you are writing
your life story not just for your friends and family, but also for
the wide world—and, if you're fortunate, for generations to come.

The simple facts of setting and time are never enough. For
example, it's not enough to just say, "It was in a tumultuous
1960 Paris that I first met . . ." or "When my pilgrim ancestors
landed on Plymouth Rock in 1620 . . ." These basic facts must
be expanded and embellished with vibrant scenes that bring
that place and time alive in exacting and exhilarating detail.

Sometimes it helps to storyboard your life, the way a screen-writer illustrates scenes in a script. By imagining the cinematic and theatrical elements of your story, you never forget that every character on a stage or a movie set must be so fully realized that the reader, too, "struts and frets his hour upon a stage," as Hamlet says in his famous soliloquy.

There are, in fact, some memoirs in which place is one of the main characters. In the best seller *Angela's Ashes*, Frank McCourt as an impoverished Irish Catholic boy is all but overwhelmed by the grind and grit of his Limerick slum. Such was McCourt's childhood imprisonment that the reader wonders at how he ever escaped such physical, societal, and cultural confinements to write this memoir. It didn't happen overnight. McCourt began what he called his "scribbling" as a child, but it wasn't until he was sixty-four, after teaching high school in the United States for decades, that he wrote *Angela's Ashes*.

The book was worth the wait. McCourt's surprising wit and lively portraits—of his parents, the priests, schoolteachers, and shopkeepers—all bring Limerick alive on the stage. McCourt is so specific about setting that in one chapter he describes how after the first floor of their house is flooded and the family must move upstairs, they decide to name their ruined first floor "Ireland" and their warm, snug second floor "Italy."

It took McCourt almost an entire lifetime to write his story. In William Zinsser's classic *Inventing the Truth: The Art and Craft of Memoir*, McCourt explains: "you can't write about that kind of childhood until you're mature enough, until you have some self-esteem." One of the ways we develop self-esteem is by knowing who and where we come from. What if you were adopted or come from a family line broken by war or slavery or exile? How do you find your place in your own life story?

GENEALOGY AND ANCESTORS AS YOUR GROUND

According to neuroscientists May-Britt and Edvard Moser, a Norwegian wife-and-husband research team, a sense of where you are—a built-in navigation system of sorts—is hardwired into the brain as "grid cells." This might explain why we feel unsettled and find it hard to concentrate and follow a memoir when place isn't well established. We're literally lost and wandering off the grid. (See Chapter Notes, page 253, for an article on this research.)

We need place information to navigate. From an early age, most of us get our grounding in place and time through our own senses and from other people. We orient ourselves by our parents and grandparents, our aunts and uncles. Through their histories, we link to our ancestors and develop a sense of continuum or time. If this isn't provided, we have no base and no solid ground, and we feel cut off and disconnected, as if constantly needing to invent who and where we are.

Until very recently, this was the experience of Jarvis Jay Masters, author of *Finding Freedom* and of the extraordinary memoir *That Bird Has My Wings*, a book that was nominated for a PEN Literary Award. While Jarvis is still imprisoned in San Quentin State Prison, many people, including Sarah Jane, believe he is innocent. In a telephone conversation Sarah Jane had with Jarvis (he is allotted a certain number of collect calls per month), Jarvis told her about his experiences with Ancestry.com. Sarah Jane was so moved by what he said about his discoveries that she asked Jarvis to send her a card describing the encounter. Jarvis writes:

> Not even a year ago, I hadn't known my grandparent's [sic] names, let alone my great-grandparent's [sic]. But now, as I learn about my ancestors going back five generations, I keep saying, "Is this real?"

To see actual photos of the slave houses they lived in; the cotton fields where they planted and picked; and seeing the family tree up to my eventual birth is beyond words. *This is where I came from—this is what made me.*

Knowing this grounds me and gives me a narrative. It allows me to speak in the first person with a confidence I never had before. If you don't know where and who you came from, you can't have any confidence about who you are now. Now, I can speak about my roots, my history in America.

You know, I never understood how empowering this is. Some days I walk around the prison exercise yard just thinking what it must have been like for my great-great-great grandfather named Streeter. Did he ever ask these questions? Did he ever come up with answers? Or, would it please him to know that I am asking these questions today—for him.

Even though Jarvis is in prison, he finds a larger territory for his life in discovering his ancestral history. "His story" is rooted for the first time in five generations of time, family, and country. This is the foundation for him to rebuild his own story. These ancestors give him the "grid cells" to navigate anew.

YOUR BOOK IS A HOUSE AND A HOME

In many ways, writing a book is like building a home. First, you carefully excavate the ground, then you lay a firm foundation, then add story upon story. A house is like the stage set for your story. Every memoirist is a home builder. And after all the years of remodeling and designing your house, you then must open it— and invite the world to move in.

As Howard Mansfield writes in his remarkable book *Dwelling in Possibility: Searching for the Soul of Shelter*, "When we belong to

Writing a book is like building a home.

a place, we dwell." If you don't give your story a dwelling place, you risk losing many readers who are grounded in place and time. Those readers will feel lost and disoriented. Your story will lack that quality of self-possession and belonging that is so vital to the foundation of a good memoir.

The idea of a book as a house is a good prompt when you're writing memoir. One of the exercises Brenda gives her students is to thoroughly describe every floor of the house in which the childhood or the drama is taking place. Some students have gone so far as to build balsa wood replicas or dollhouses, or to draft intricate blueprints. Others, with more of an eye to interior design, will scrounge around in Goodwill or antique stores to find just that right old-fashioned lampshade, or colorful hand-knit rag rug, or wicker rocking chair that summons up a remembered setting for them. By having such touchstones to another time and place, writers feel more rooted in and transported to *that* real world and can bring back more authentic stories from it.

THE SENSUAL WRITER

How do you remember a scene from your life? Do you remember the colors, the sounds, or the touch of someone's hand? How you reconstruct a scene will be very much based on your primary senses. If, like Brenda, your most developed sense is sound, and then touch, you might remember extended dialogues and all of the body language, but not notice what someone was wearing or the scent of perfume. If you are, like most people, very visual, you may remember the exact slant of summer light in a scene or the layout of a house; but you can't recall what you ate, the surprising dinner conversation, or the splinters of the porch swing.

Be in touch with *all* of your senses—it's what will make your writing exciting and colorful and real. Smell, hear, touch, and taste but don't overuse the fifth sense—sight. It is the sense which is most obvious and often less evocative than the other four. Identify your primary and secondary senses, and then also write from the senses that are less developed for you. Some people claim that awareness or intuition is the sixth sense.

When you do these exercises below, don't concentrate on the obvious, such as the robust smell of coffee, or the silken feel of water, or the echo of Tibetan bells, or the pungent taste of curry. Be specific and acutely aware of how each sense enlivens a scene. And remember, do not just focus on your sense of sight.

Smell

Don't simply describe the general scent; go a little deeper to the more subtle aromas. Patrick Suskind's entire novel, *Perfume*, is an erotic feast of fragrances. Smells can conjure up an entire universe and open the doors to a flood of evocative memories.

WRITING PROMPT: Before I saw her face, I caught her scent—a surprising waft of _____.

Touch

Of course, there's always the memory of being touched connected with a lover. But go a little deeper: how about the gritty sand sinking underfoot on a beach? Or the rivulets of sweat running down your back? Or the mineral glory of an Italian spa's sulfur mud bath.

WRITING PROMPT: If I were blind, I would remember his face with my hands. The curve of his high brow felt like _____.

Taste

There are countless warm taste memories that summon your mom's fabulous chestnut-and-celery turkey stuffing, your grandmother's blackberry cobbler, or the way lemon meringue tart lingers on the tongue. But what about when you were embarrassed into tasting your first slimy oyster or when you wanted to be a grown-up and took a swallow of gin or Jack Daniels and thought it tasted like medicine you wanted to spit out? Perhaps the unpleasant taste memories will take you to a more interesting place.

WRITING PROMPT: How could chocolate and chili not tantalize me when I tasted my first _____? Or, When I finally tasted _____, I _____.

Hearing

Hearing is our first and last sense, so evolution dictates just how vital this sense is for our survival. It's also important for our storytelling. Have you ever noticed that little boys make a lot of noises when they tell their first stories—*whiz, pow, bang, pop!*—while little girls often have a more subtle and quiet soundtrack? Perhaps girls are discouraged from being too bold and brassy while boys are rewarded for noisier king-of-the-mountain monologues. But as we point out in the chapter "The Music of Memoir," the listening ear is physiologically a more feminine instrument than the more masculine eye. So female writers should naturally have an edge when it comes to the sound of their stories.

Close your eyes right now and listen intently to the sounds surrounding you. Your body, especially your skin, is always hearing and responding to vibrations all around: Electric fan. Traffic. Surf. Foghorns. Barking dogs. Lawn mower. Ticking timer. Birdsong. Radio. Describe these sounds in detail, using language that is alive and rhythmic, to echo the acoustic experience in words. Be like the classical percussionist Evelyn Glennie, who is deaf but feels sound vibrating in her body as she makes her remarkable music.

Synesthesia

Why not mingle *all* of your senses to create unusual and original metaphors or images? Hear colors. Touch sounds. Taste light. Smell music. Many artists use synesthesia, such as novelist Vladimir Nabokov or writer Diane Ackerman, who writes in *An Alchemy of Mind*, "Sensory details fascinate me, and always have . . . I was born a sensualist . . . I'm a synesthete." Ackerman, whose language is both playful and radiantly alive, notes that synesthesia occurs seven times more often among artists.

One of Brenda's favorite writing exercises to stretch the mind and senses is what she calls "Forced Relationships," in which two wildly unrelated objects must be linked to find a common ground.

WRITING PROMPTS FOR FORCED RELATIONSHIPS: How is a cloud like a coat hanger? How is a reptile like a computer? How is a cat like a church steeple? How is a hat like a pressure cooker? How is a lamp like a pie? How is a necklace like a sausage? How is a rug like a baseball bat? How is a tree like a gold doubloon?

WRITING PROMPTS FOR SYNESTHESIA: What color is B-flat? When you touch the color orange, what do you feel on your fingertips? What does rose quartz sound like? What is the exact fragrance of that shaft of sunlight on your desk? Can you taste turquoise?

WRITING PROMPTS FOR COMPLEX SENTENCES: Write a five-page biography of your life, using the most complicated sentences you can create. For example, don't just write: "I was born in 1960 in Ames, Iowa." Instead, write: "In Amish country, there were midwives who would still come by horseback to our farmhouse, even in 1960, when I was born in Ames, Iowa."

NATURE IS A "DOOR ONTO ANOTHER SELF"

Some memoirists find their sense of home or territory in nature, not in any man-made dwellings. "I like to say that I was babysat by nature," Alice Walker told an interviewer.

Terry Tempest Williams finds refuge in the wilds of Mormon Utah and the Great Salt Lake basin. In *Refuge: An Unnatural History of Family and Place*, she writes eloquently of her homeland's wildlife, especially birds, the craggy canyons, and vast vistas. She notes that she "was raised to believe in a spirit world . . . And if the natural world was assigned spiritual values, then those days spent in wildness were sacred."

Nature writing is a particular tributary of memoir that ironically has gained prominence even as we seem fully engaged in destroying our planet. If you are ever in doubt about what tack to take next in a chapter, consider the natural world. It is everybody's setting. Nature is much more than simply a backdrop for our human dramas. It has its own story. The seas, land, forests, animals, and even rocks have stories that must be told.

One of the most celebrated memoirs that uses place as a main character is Annie Dillard's *Pilgrim at Tinker Creek*. Consciously setting out in the tradition of Henry David Thoreau's New England masterpiece, *Walden*, Dillard explores one creek in Virginia over one summer—yet through this natural microcosm, she travels the universe. "It has always been a happy thought to me that the creek runs on all night," she writes, "new every minute, whether I wish it or know it or care, as a closed book on a shelf continues to whisper to itself its own inexhaustible tale." What might happen if you simply told the story of a daylighted stream in your neighborhood, or a clear-cut forest, or a flood, or one island's tsunami or hurricane (think Japan or Manhattan)? What life story might you tell if your setting was as much a companion to you as any person?

"IT WAS THE BEST OF TIMES, IT WAS THE WORST OF TIMES"

For some, a memoir is set during a time or place of excitement or even exhilaration; for others, it is a retelling of a terrible moment or revolution. Charles Dickens's famous opening line to *A Tale of Two Cities* suggests that it is always the best and the worst of times, often simultaneously. Sarah Jane notes that of the many submissions she receives, most narrate a difficult passage: sexual or emotional abuse, surviving illness or divorce, a country at war or suffering disaster. Brenda tries to balance the suffering by teaching her students to write as many love scenes as death scenes—the latter are actually much easier to write. Fortunately, these best and worst stories can both make for good reading, but only if you tell the story with some balance, perspective, not a shard of self-pity, and with an eye to presenting that larger world and time.

To re-create a specific time, it helps to immerse yourself in it so fully it's as if you're living a double life: your life in the present and your life in whatever time period you're creating on the page. Some writers like to make elaborate models using magazines of the time period. For example, when one of Brenda's students was writing a memoir set in the Great Depression, she rented movies like *The Grapes of Wrath*, based on John Steinbeck's classic novel, or Ken Burns's remarkable film documentary *The Dust Bowl*. She printed out color photos from online and library archives, pasting them up on one wall in her study. Every day at her desk whenever her mind and eye would wander, she'd settle on a photo of a dust storm rising up over barren farmland; or a dilapidated farmhouse; or Margaret Bourke-White portraits of homeless Depression-era wanderers. (See Chapter Notes, page 253, for a web link to Margaret Bourke-White's photos.) Steeped in such stories and imagery, she was able to describe the desolation of the American 1930s with a sensual grasp of both time and prairie:

That spring of 1935, she grew used to the granular taste of dirt in all she ate, the prickling sand in her bed, her clothes, permanent grit scabbing her scalp. For miles around there was nothing but ridged, windswept desert where once were her fields. The last storm was a churning, filthy tidal wave, its billows high over the black horizon, as if the Rocky Mountains had disintegrated, blown here like flotsam.

TIME TRAVEL: FAST-FORWARDS AND FLASHBACKS

Flashbacks are a detaching from present reality to add another dimension: the past. Just as you imagine a stage as a setting, think of time as a clothesline stretched throughout your memoir. This timeline should be taut and dramatic. If the clothesline is too burdened with disorienting flashbacks—interior, big building blocks of backstory—it will sag, and so will your main story.

When you flash back in time, all forward movement, or plot, stops. It is like hanging a heavy fur coat on that clothesline. Don't let your timeline drag and your clothesline droop with the weight of the past. Be very conscious of how many times you interrupt the present action to slip away into the past. Don't undermine your story with asking the reader to zip around crazily between past and present. Each flashback should be consciously crafted, because that's the way your nonchronological mind is working. Be careful of every beginning writer's problem: *flashbackitis* and lost in time.

Remember in *Star Trek* when Captain Kirk commands, "Beam me up!"? Before he shifts between places or times, he first sets coordinates. The way a writer can set these coordinates is through a physical detail that is so real the reader won't mind time travel.

Fiction writers often do this more successfully than memoirists, who are often so stuck in the past that almost their whole books are flashbacks.

In a seamless mini-flashback, in *After Rain*, author William Trevor shows his heroine, Harriet, dining alone. Her elegant supper of Gorgonzola and pecorino cheeses, wine, chicken, roast potatoes, tomatoes, and salad are sensory details that ground the reader securely in what will happen next: a breathtaking flashback:

> She folds her napkin and tucks it away, and for a moment as she does so the man she has come here to forget pushes through another crowded room, coming towards her . . . her name on his lips. 'I love you, Harriet,' he whispers beneath the noise around them.

Just as suddenly as we are flashed back to this romantic moment, Trevor returns us to the present, and Harriet is alone again. The next paragraph begins, "Upstairs, in the room where the bookcases are, Harriet wonders if this solitude is how her life will be." Trevor doesn't plunge the reader back into the past very long. With the speed of a boomerang, which is how the brain and memories work, Trevor throws us back to the very memory that his character is trying to escape. He trusts that the past happiness is even more powerful when it haunts the present.

This conscious crafting of time is what can make a memoir as lively as a novel. To study the expert use of flashbacks, read more fiction. Like a novelist, think of opening a chapter with a high point of action, then a flashback. Before asking your readers to time-travel, give them strong sensory coordinates in the present so that they can find their way back.

Many writers are fond of exclusively using present tense in their memoirs, as if to suggest timeliness and "you are here with me right now." You can gain a sense of immediacy, stream of consciousness, and spontaneity when you use present tense. But you are also limiting yourself in terms of flashing around in time. There is a reason why the simple past works best in most stories. In past tense, you are free to use flashbacks and fast-forwards with ease—and without disorienting the reader.

In past tense, there is also a steadiness and master-storyteller voice that allows the reader to come closer to your narrative tone, instead of grabbing the reader with a show of just how *now-now-now* your story is. Sarah Jane and Brenda both prefer the elegance and many options of past tense, especially in memoir; because it offers—even in the verbs—a sense of reflection and maturity. Past tense grounds the reader in time so they can pay attention to everything else that is going on in your life story.

Brenda often talks to her students about the pitfalls of "no time," in memoir. This is when writers are wandering in narration, without any scenes to orient them. On every page, as you write, you should be able to answer these questions:

Where am I in time and space? What setting?
What is my body doing?
What is the weather? What time period am I in?

When you veer away from the active scenes of your storyline for flashbacks, you often abandon any sense of setting. Imagine if you were watching a play and suddenly a master of ceremonies leapt onstage and droned on about the characters' pasts, their backgrounds, their interior lives. You'd be very bored and soon frustrated with the fact that all action has stopped, frozen in time while the narrator is grandstanding onstage. His distracting dominance would seem at best dissociative—and at worst, indifferent to the poor actors waiting for their story to move on.

Whether deeply rooting your life story in your home, leaving home, or searching to find home, your setting is always the home of your book. Inhabit it fully.

PUBLISHING TIPS

A hill is a house for an ant, an ant.
A hive is a house for a bee.
~**MARY ANN HOBERMAN FROM *A HOUSE IS A HOUSE FOR ME***

With images such as "A rose is a house for a smell" and "A book is a house for a story," a sense of belonging and order and having everything in its place in a sometimes topsy-turvy world was what Sarah Jane loved about the children's book *A House Is a House for Me*. Knowing where things are in space and time is calming and reassuring for young, old, and in between. Sarah Jane says that while she's open to reading an author whose writing is impressionistic, spacious, or even stream of consciousness, she wants a work to be really specific about when and where events take place. Rather than leaving your readers dislocated and trying to figure where in heaven's name we are, please provide those essential details of place so that we can enjoy the writing and relax into your story.

Exercises: Diagramming a Scene

Think of yourself as a master builder constructing your book like a house. Each story may be a section of your life. Or each house may be a part of your memoir. Visually organize your life into stories of a house. Use photos and storyboards.

Construct a replica of the house in which your life story takes place. Draw it, photograph it, and build a dollhouse version of it,

What country, land, river, ocean, or island is also a main character in your life story?

Play "Animal, Vegetable, and Mineral" with your own character? What animal are you? What body of water? What forest? What country? What wilderness?

What landscape most haunts or troubles you? Why?

What country, tradition, or culture is a setting and backdrop for all of your stories?

More Writing Prompts

There is one place on earth that is my sanctuary, and that is _____.

When I am in _____, I know I am home.

I am in my element whenever I visit _____.

The backdrop to all of my favorite scenes is _____.

If I could choose only one setting for my life, it would be _____.

My memories of that time in _____ are the most vivid.

The decade when I was the most "awake" is _____. The decade I barely remember is _____. The decade I never want to endure again is _____.

7.
EAT, PRAY, LOVE

It seems to me that our three basic needs, for food and security and love, are so mixed and mingled and entwined that we cannot straightly think of one without the others.

~M. F. K. FISHER, *THE ART OF EATING*

Sarah Jane often remarks that if she had a dollar for every memoir pitched to her that begins "My memoir is a cross between *Eat, Pray, Love* and [fill in the blank]," she'd be able to spend a year just walking on beaches around the world. While none of the submissions were anything like *Eat, Pray, Love*, ideally they should, in fact, address those three subjects.

EAT

Because it's fun and essential and something we all do, often with others, your memoir should address your relationship with food. Do you love and enjoy food or fear it? Is it simply fuel? Have you felt fed and nourished, or not? Some of us had mothers who devotedly (or frustratingly) spent all their time in the kitchen. Others had mothers who never fed them much more than Twinkies. Writing about food humanizes us and creates an immediate link that we can connect to and relish.

Sarah Jane represents many successful food writers, like Paula Wolfert, John Ash, and Aglaia Kremezi. She often advises *all* of her authors to include a recipe—even if their books are not about food, and even if the recipe doesn't end up in the finished work. She once advised an author that her book should be in the same vein as Ilene Beckerman's book *Love, Loss, and What I Wore*, except it should be called *Love, Loss, and What I Cooked*. It seems all of the author's relationships could be seen from the vantage point of food and what she cooked for the various men in her life. From food, her whole story unfolded.

But even for those of us who are not so food-focused, eating is so obviously a part of our lives that writing about it can uncover multiple levels of insight. (See Chapter 13, "'Foodoirs' and Feeding the Hungry Writer," for more on food memoirs, and even a recipe.)

Exercise: The Main Dish

Write about a meal or dish from your childhood. Reflect upon who made it, where you ate it, what you were feeling, or what you believe the one who prepared it (or with whom you ate it) was feeling. Was it someone you loved and need to thank? Or someone who needs to be forgiven? Or someone whose cooking you want to preserve for future generations?

Many of the most intriguing and successful memoirs, are, in fact, food-related. Family meals are the subject of many of the most beautiful, poignant, and revealing scenes in any memoir. When in doubt, tell a story set at the dinner table, or a picnic, or a wake.

Another good exercise is actually to re-create a dish, or if you are really ambitious, an entire meal. Don't buy it ready-made. Make it yourself from scratch. If you haven't eaten that particular dish in ages, better yet.

No matter what your
story, write about food.

Maybe you'll be learning for the first time what it takes to prepare it. Maybe you'll have to call a relative to see if he or she remembers how.

Once you've perfected the recipe, share it with someone. See how it feels to feed someone a dish from your childhood. You will taste your childhood—and someone else will, too. This will make both of you happy and may evoke forgotten memories or trigger new ones. In her memoir *I Want to Be Left Behind,* Brenda celebrates the "revelation" of her mother's homemade ice cream and the fact that in the fervent Southern Baptist socials of her childhood, food was love, a reason to keep coming to church: "Who could resist the temptation of wild blackberry cobbler . . . or the church ladies' triple-fudge brownies studded with glazed pecans?" And for "backsliders" or "shut-ins" who didn't attend church socials, there were progressive dinners, which were "basically pious pig-outs." From house to house, the faithful trooped together, sampling appetizers, salads, side dishes, hearty smoked hams, and barbecued meat, completed by "a Roman debauch of desserts." The whole menu of one such extravagant progressive dinner Brenda jotted down in her adolescent diary and memoir.

Sarah Jane remembers most her mother's rice pudding. To this day, neither she nor her two sisters know the recipe. While their mother was not motherly or nurturing, hers was the creamiest, richest, most comforting rice pudding imaginable. Why not whip up your favorite childhood recipe and a story to garnish it? And on your writing shrine, place an offering of something sweet. Hindus call such an offering *prasad.* It is a precious gift, usually an edible food, offered to a deity.

EAT: PUBLISHING TIPS

No matter what your story, write about food. There is no tale so weird, so scaring, or so joyous that food doesn't play a role. In fact, the more unusual or ordinary your story, the more vital the subject of food is. Food keeps it real. Even the epic medieval high-fantasy A Game of Thrones series became the inspiration for a cookbook that has sold thousands of copies.

One of the reasons Elizabeth Gilbert's *Eat, Pray, Love* was such a best seller was that it was divided into three simple sections, which readers could understand and track along with her. Gilbert had already committed to a narrative arc that was easily understood by editors. In fact, the publisher was supporting Gilbert with a book advance (against royalties) throughout her travels. It was as if Gilbert was on a kind of journalistic "junket" or tour of her own life's aspirations. As a travel writer and journalist, Gilbert was writing her *outer* journey, replete with exotic settings. But she was also writing her *inner* journey. And food was a major theme in all of it.

Rena Kornreich Gelissen, a young woman from Poland, was sent on the first Jewish transport to Auschwitz in 1942. In her amazing 1995 memoir, *Rena's Promise* (written with the help of Heather Dune Macadam), some of the most painful and redemptive stories are about food—the food Rena and her younger sister, Danka, just barely survive on in the concentration camp, and the food Rena remembered from her happy childhood. In one of the most poignant scenes, Rena writes about how she and Danka risked their lives for a small piece of bread thrown over a fence to them by a young man:

> Huddled next to each other we divide the bread. This is not the sawdust-and-water biscuit-shit we get from the Germans, this is heavy Polish bread that comes from the earth and has been

kneaded by a farm woman's hands . . . There is a memory that surfaces just behind my eyes, something about bread and Mama.

While lecturing on the Holocaust at a university, Rena was asked what the most painful experience of the camps was. She replied: "The hunger."

Whether it's the hot dog you wolfed down at a ball game with your dad, the weird Jell-O molds your mom created, or the *panna cotta* you shared with your lover, food is a universal language. It evokes the nostalgia of childhood, the discovery of travel, and the promise of seduction. It also evokes the pain of hunger—both physical and emotional. Sharing food, like music, is universal and transcends every psychological, cultural, and emotional barrier. So please, remember to invite your readers to break bread with you.

PRAY

Have you rejected, abandoned, returned to, or nurtured your faith? Or taken on a different one? Exploring your beliefs is one of the major elements of any memoir. Can you remember your earliest spiritual memory? Was it sad or amusing? Did it open doorways into your evolution as a soul and a writer?

Often we think that because we're writing about our spiritual experiences, it means that we are supposed to write "spiritually" and abandon all sense of humor. The most common mistake when writing a spiritual memoir is to become endlessly ecstatic and self-involved. It's like reading about someone's dreams—usually only interesting to the dreamer, a good friend, or an analyst.

Authors who write most successfully and inspiringly about their spiritual lives are those who are able to convey a spiritual message without becoming overly religious or dogmatic. In fact, spirituality is more often shown in very specific, humble, and ordinary things.

Brenda is always telling her students: "The more metaphysical your story, the more physical." Flights into nirvana or enlightenment are usually unreadable, unless they are grounded in everyday details and experience. And "channeled" books need to channel a very good editor. Sarah Jane calls such memoirs "the work of spiritual space cadets."

You can't just write, "And then I knew that love was love and all was love." Or, "I realized suddenly that I was not alone. That I was One with All."

Even if these moments of oneness or loving union are what we all search for, they must be told with a setting, a body, an emotion, and even perhaps other characters besides the initiate. They must entertain, as well as enlighten us.

Sarah Jane notes that among her authors who write memoir, many of them write about the things they do—not just their spiritual life. There's a reason so many books have to do with cooking, gardening, or some other daily practice. The writer and teacher Elizabeth Mattis-Namgyel, in her book *The Power of an Open Question: The Buddha's Path to Freedom*, uses rock climbing and horseback riding as her métiers for memoir. Using climbing as a metaphor for a spiritual path is very effective, because it connects to something material and real.

Try starting with something small that you take for granted, like your garden or your kitchen or your bicycle. It's what you do effortlessly that is often very important.

Exercise: Keep Silent

Spiritual experiences are so powerful that they often defy our ability to describe them. As an exercise, Sarah Jane suggests keeping silent. Don't talk, don't write, don't even journal. Allow yourself just to "be." How about trying it for a weekend? Better yet, go, if you can, on a silent retreat. By the end of the retreat, you'll be amazed at how renewed and peaceful you feel. You will experience yourself and your stories in a new and refreshing way. You may even have moments of understanding rise up, seemingly without any will or effort.

On your shrine, place an object that represents spirit or silence.

PRAY: PUBLISHING TIPS

Of the three experiential avenues, "Pray" might be the trickiest because one's tendency could be either to overlook spirituality or to become overly zealous. As you write your memoir, maybe you think "Pray" is relevant only to those who are religious, who believe in a god and who actually, in the traditional sense, pray. Not so. Call it what you will, but "Pray" is about beliefs and faith and spirit (with or without a god) and readers will want to know about this dimension of you. We all believe in something, so what about you? Do you believe in courage, honesty, beauty, and maybe God? Or are you passionately antireligious, like the late Christopher Hitchens, who wrote *God Is Not Great: How Religion Poisons Everything*, and, after he discovered he had inoperable cancer, *Mortality*? Hitchens remained firm and never faltered in his agnosticism, even when faced with certain death. And yes, that too is "Pray."

Those of you who have had religious or spiritual experiences, beware of being overly fervent or simply mouthing empty generalities. Make sure you don't write from such a lofty position that you lose touch with your (and our) common humanity. The more profound your experience and deeper your understanding, the more your writing should expand to encompass even the minutiae of this world. If you make us aware of the extraordinary nature of the ordinary, if you write with nuance and detail, it will ensure that your writing will rise above the generic.

Remember Brenda's rule: The more spiritual your memoir, the more specific and down-to-earth it must be—because a book is not a pulpit or a persuasion or a conversion experience. It is an engaging story more about the search and the seeker than the answers.

Our somewhat tongue-in-cheek rule is: be reverent about your nonbelief and irreverent about your belief.

LOVE

Do you remember the first time you fell in love? Or the most recent? That giddy, swept-up-in-a-whirlwind, billowy, intense, and vulnerable feeling? It's as if every moment with your beloved is etched in your brain. Senses are heightened, and you reflect over and over on every physical detail, every scrap of dialogue, and every hint of uncertainty, possible loss, or betrayal. And then, of course, there are the ghosts of past relationships chatting away in your head. Sometimes it seems that there are many others in the bed with you and your lover.

In memoir, who or what we love is often the passion that fuels the story. Loves found and loves lost are like engines propelling the story forward. So discovering who or what you love is a primal force in writing memoir. Of course, the same might be said for hate, but writing out of hatred is not as interesting or even as fulfilling as writing from some shade of love. Also, readers are very quick to resent or abandon a memoir that is nothing more than thinly disguised "blame-and-shame." For every *Mommie Dearest*, there is a much more enduring *Glass Castle* or *When I Was Puerto Rican*.

No one wants to read your personal rant. And while a mem oir can be cathartic for you, and can even right wrongs, it cannot be an act of vengeance. If it is, it will spread pain all around and neither you, nor anyone reading it, will benefit. If you don't understand why someone, often a family member, acted the way they did or said what they said, pretend to—until you actually do. Write in their voice, from their perspective, and you might discover an empathic love you never knew you had.

When Brenda worked in the editorial offices of the *New Yorker* in her twenties, she often typed up correspondence from the great E. B. White, whose many essays and children's books have enthralled readers for decades. One of his fan letters was from a little girl who scrawled in careful cursive across a piece of jumbo-size paper:

Dear E. B. White,
I love you for writing *Charlotte's Web*!

Exercise: The First Face You Ever Loved

Can you remember and describe the first face you ever loved? It might surprise you. It might not be a parent, but a babysitter or a grandparent. Or it might be that of a beloved animal or an author or sibling or a character from a book. Hold this image in your mind and bring it to life using all of your senses: sight, touch, taste, smell, and hearing. Then add a sixth sense of intuition.

Let the reader also fall in love with this remembered face. And follow it through your whole story. Think of this face as a kind of touchstone or guide as you write. On your shrine, place a photo or drawing or word portrait of the first face you ever loved.

Sometimes discovering what we truly love is one of the greatest gifts of writing memoir. When Brenda began *Build Me an Ark*, she gave herself and her students the "What was the first face you ever loved?" exercise. Her answer to this seemingly simple question was revelatory. Brenda discovered that she had first imprinted on the deer-head trophies that hung above her crib in the US Forest Service cabin where her family lived:

> Sometimes my father would lift me up to run my hands over the tanned fur of these deer, the first faces I ever loved; I touched the long slope of jawbones and sensitive snouts, the pricked ears and tufts at the top of their heads. Most amazing were the antlers—I expected I would grow my own someday.

LOVE: PUBLISHING TIPS

Here is what both of us know about writing a book, publishing a book, and love: no agent ever represented a book unless she or he first fell in love with it. Sure, there are various other considerations, but unless there's love, the writer is going to get one of those "Sorry, it's not for us" letters.

In addition, no book was ever published unless an *editor* first fell in love with it. It isn't until the corporate machine gets involved (with its sales forecasts, production estimates, distribution costs, and marketing considerations) that an editor must intellectually justify and defend an author's submission. Until then, it's all about love.

And it doesn't matter if a book is published traditionally or online, it cannot be successful unless readers fall in love and tell all their friends that they will fall in love, too.

Simply put—it is love that gets your book represented and sold and makes it a success. You have to write about love, even if you're a tough cookie and as hard as nails, or a sentimental softie. Don't limit the reader's experience; enrich and enhance your story with love. Consider love in all its manifestations: passion, tenderness, infatuation, adoration, intimacy, yearning, devotion, and even obsession.

> *And now these three remain: faith, hope, and*
> *love. But the greatest of these is love.*
> ~1 CORINTHIANS 13:13, THE NEW TESTAMENT

Writing Prompts

A revealing recipe for my life is _____.

When I pray, I find myself _____.

Food in my family was _____.

If I hadn't first loved _____, my life would have _____.

Whenever I eat _____, I remember _____.

My own recipe for enlightenment is _____.

My soul's journey is _____.

The love of my life really is _____.

8.
TRAVEL MEMOIRS: JOURNEYS IN AND OUT

---

*There is a land called Crete in the midst
of the wine-dark sea . . .*

~HOMER, *THE ODYSSEY*

The time-honored tradition of writing about travel goes all the way back to Homer's iconic *The Odyssey*, and in the oral tradition, far earlier. What, after all, is a more apt metaphor for life than the journey—whether it involves actually going on the road or happens while still at home? Travel puts you on new ground and means you can't follow your familiar daily routine. Like Ariel sings in Shakespeare's *The Tempest*, you will "suffer a sea-change" that will carry you out of the habits of your everyday life and challenge you to become more aware and more attentive. Of course, you could journey to the ends of the earth and not have your perspective changed one iota; or like Eckhart Tolle, author of *The Power of Now: A Guide to Spiritual Enlightenment*, you could simply walk around the corner and be jolted into seeing the world through new eyes.

Travel memoirs are not only popular; they are also never out of fashion. What armchair traveler doesn't adore slipping through the portal into another's astonishing adventure? Bruce Chatwin, the uber–travel writer and author of *What Am I Doing Here*, writes that "Man's real home is not a house but the Road, and that life itself is a journey to be walked on foot." (Or boat, or train, or camel, or balloon, or kayak.)

Recently, Sarah Jane and a few friends went sailing in the Bahamas from one uninhabited island to another. Every day they'd leave the large yacht anchored offshore and climb into a small dinghy to get a closer look at wherever they were. On one such trip, as they were trying to decide which of the stunning pink- and white-sand beaches to explore, they asked, "Where shall we go?" In response, Sarah Jane suddenly remembered the wonderful thing a young friend had recently said: "Go where you're loved."

Going where you're loved can involve a momentous decision like which agent should represent your book, or it could mean going on a heritage-seeking trip in search of your roots and being welcomed by distant relatives you didn't know you had. Sarah Jane has realized that "going where you're loved" is what motivates most of her travels. Although there are many places in this world she'd like to visit, this maxim makes the choice much easier.

From her vantage point on that boat in the Bahamas, through experiencing the excitement of exploring the next coral reef (hopefully, sans sharks or barracudas), tasting the next fresh fish, and seeing the next glowing sunset or luminous night sky, Sarah Jane discovered that she better understands the enthusiasm with which would-be clients send her their wanderlust manuscripts. These memoirs chronicle a writer who goes somewhere exotic, eats unusual food at weird and remarkable restaurants, meets all manner of odd and interesting characters—and hikes, bikes, climbs, treks, swims, sails, and flies here, there, and everywhere.

What is a more apt metaphor
for life than the journey?

Many of Brenda's students are veteran travelers. On any given week in her evening class of ten students, five of them may be far-flung, in the Amazon, Namibia, Nepal, Italy, China, or Japan. Many of these writers are at work on memoirs set in foreign lands, calling upon the journals of their younger days in the Peace Corps, or anthropological research in Malaysia, or a CIA assignment in Turkey. One of Brenda's students, a therapist and devoted traveler, often quotes her flight instructor: "How can you be lost if you don't care where you are?" Brenda's best friend, Rebecca Romanelli, has traveled extensively in the third world, often alone. "When I travel, I become more than myself, my habits, or my limitations," Rebecca notes. "Travel is like an instant awakening process. It forces you to be present in the moment and explore *other* people's realities."

Surrounded by such avid travel correspondents, Brenda enjoys following an elder friend's dictum: "Never leave home!" Brenda is not an exuberant traveler—and yet she has traveled all her life. Her nomadic childhood, following her father's US Forest Service work, meant Brenda lived in diverse regions of the United States— from the West to the South to New England. Moving on the average of every two years made Brenda a perpetual "new girl" at school and left her with a permanent sense of culture shock. The writerly benefit of such radical movement is that from an early age, Brenda learned to develop her memory to re-create what she had loved and left. It also made her more observant and keenly aware of how shifts in place don't necessarily change one's inner life. The so-called "baggage" that therapists are always talking about is often carried inside, no matter where we travel. Yet sometimes that inner baggage is transformed by carrying it outward into the wider world. And *that* is the story.

TRAVELING FROM THE INSIDE OUT

In her thirties, a midlife crisis crept up on Sarah Jane. Eventually, tired of herself and her constant tristesse, she accepted an invitation to go to India and Kashmir with a group of meditators she had befriended. Sarah Jane hoped that this journey would give her the opportunity to explore a new self and see herself in another light. And she was right. Most importantly, she discovered that shining even through her sadness was a certain joie de vivre and sense of fun. Like so many of the writers we work with, through travel she discovered an inner strength and an affirmation of life. This connection between travel, inner discovery, and growth is what makes a travel memoir riveting.

Cheryl Strayed's successful memoir, *Wild: From Lost to Found on the Pacific Crest Trail*, is a poignant and brave blend of this inner and outer journey. Grieving her mother's death and lost marriage, Strayed felt she had nothing left to lose. So she set out on an eleven-hundred-mile hike from the Mojave Desert through California, Oregon, and Washington. She was alone, and at one point, barefoot, without hiking boots. Her reassuring opening line sets the theme for the whole memoir: "The trees were tall, but I was taller." She's immediately signaling to the reader that though the hike was often dangerous and overwhelming, and sometimes she was "the only girl in the woods," she would prevail. In Strayed's memoir, we understand that the wilderness is also *within* her. Strayed uses grief as a touchstone. It is the catalyst but *not* the path, not the organizing principle. Grief is not her ground; wilderness is.

When Strayed was teaching a workshop at Centrum in Port Townsend, Washington, after *Wild* had become an Oprah's Book Club phenomenon, she commented about how she carefully constructed her memoir. Despite her last name, her writing never strayed far from the trail. Each chapter, she stressed, was firmly grounded on the Pacific Crest Trail, before she flashed back to any other scenes from her life. This way, the reader can almost physically accompany Strayed on her courageous and harrowing trek. So we never get lost. We hike alongside Strayed in a kind of modern-day *Pilgrim's Progress*, because her descriptions of the setting are so vivid and accessible. We move with her out of a pilgrim's "Slough of Despond" and into self-discovery.

At the end of the long trail, on one of Strayed's last days, the reader truly believes her as she squats down by a river to splash her face and wonders where the mother is that she "carried so long, staggering beneath her weight." After all, Strayed's grief had been as heavy as her backpack. The answer is as clear as the stream: "*On the other side of the river,* I let myself think. And something inside of me released."

What we carry on our travels and what we let go of is often the real story. Writing about where and how we wander is the outer journey that always needs the inner journey to make a good memoir.

BE *THERE*, NOT HERE

Several of Sarah Jane's best-selling authors are expert travelers: Stephanie Elizondo Griest writes about traveling behind the former Iron Curtain as a young woman and profiles her dangerous commute across the border in *Mexican Enough: My Life between the Borderlines*. Her book *100 Places Every Woman Should Go*, which won a Gold Prize from the Lowell Thomas Travel Journalism Competition, is a must-read for any writer contemplating a travel memoir. Griest offers lively guides to feminine sanctuaries, spas, and historical places. You can track the birthplace of Joan of Arc, revisit the Salem witchcraft trials, trek in Tibet, and sink into Japanese or Brazilian spas. "No matter where I am—downtown Manhattan or the Mongolian steppe," writes Griest, "it is inevitably in the eyes of another woman that I find a similar spark or sense of wonderment."

We also admire the anthology *A Road of Her Own: Women's Journeys in the West* by one of Brenda's favorite editors, Marlene Blessing. Move over Thelma and Louise! These are road-trip memoir pieces that don't end with women driving off a cliff. This collection includes an essay from naturalist Susan Zwinger, author of *The Last Wild Edge*, a memoir following her journey from the Arctic Circle to the ancient Hoh Rain Forest on the Olympic Peninsula of Washington State; also included is an essay from novelist Bharti Kirchner, who often writes about food and travel in her world journeys. Marlene, who celebrated her most recent birthday by traveling around the Galápagos Islands by boat, poignantly notes that earlier generations of women, especially in the West, have left us a legacy of "picaresque romps" and "wild and free" adventures that "still smile upon us as we journey along the open highways and solitary back roads of our chosen land."

For world travelers who want to take their extravagant and well-planned time as they write, Sarah Jane's author Rolf Potts wrote the very popular *Vagabonding: An Uncommon Guide to the Art of Long-Term World Travel*. In the book he explores the opportunities that arise when you take several months off from daily life to travel. He points out that the word *vagabond* is derived from Latin and refers to "a wanderer with no fixed home." One of our favorite lines from his inspiring and charming book is "Vagabonding is about gaining the courage to loosen your grip on the so-called certainties of this world." This could also describe how a writer must face the journey of creating a memoir—for just as travel changes us, so does writing a life story.

A lovely example of how travel changes one's character is the classic *No Hurry to Get Home*, a collection of articles from one of Brenda's favorite travel memoirists, Emily Hahn. At an early age, Hahn ran away from home, a presage of her famed career as one of "Our Far-Flung Correspondents" for the *New Yorker*. Hahn began writing about her travels in lively letters home to family. Her brother-in-law submitted some of these letters to a *New Yorker* editor, and that began Hahn's sixty-eight-year stint as one of the magazine's most prolific reporters. When Brenda was working at the magazine, she would always rejoice in the rare times Hahn was actually in residence in her spacious, sunlit office. Some of the best writing advice Brenda ever received was from this flame-haired, strapping, glamorous-in-spite-of-herself travel writer:

"Whatever place you're writing about, be *there*, not here," Hahn once advised Brenda in her trademark vivacious tones. "Don't read current events or newspapers; don't get distracted by what's happening right now. Throw yourself back into the exact time and place of your book. That's how the story comes alive for you and your readers."

Dutifully, Brenda took Hahn's advice. She haunted the New York Public Library, reading 1930s back issues of *Life* and *Look* and *Time* magazines, studying fashions, politics, and entertainment— all to better re-create the Depression-era South of the characters in her first novel, *River of Light*. Now, with the vast resources of the Internet, any memoirist can see video clips, online magazines, photos, and newspapers from archives, all while sitting at his or her desk. But don't forget the library, because that's where the real treasures often await.

Emily Hahn's story certainly comes alive in her travel writing. And even though it's a very specific time and place, her memoir is timeless. In "The Big Smoke," Hahn gets addicted to opium in China and describes the smell of the Chinese cookhouses as "something like burning caramel or those herbal cigarettes smoked by asthmatics." Spending Christmas in the Belgian Congo, Hahn relishes the "floating sense of unreality" as she wondered, "where exactly was I?" Anxious on an African safari, she has the epiphany "I am adaptable," and her fears ebb when she realizes "there is nothing more reassuring than to be surrounded by cowards."

Speaking for all of us who write about our travels, Hahn remarks in her memoir, "On returning from a long absence, I am always surprised and even resentful to find friends and landmarks changed. I never seem to remember that I, too, must have changed."

There are some of us who, for whatever reason, cannot physically take to the road. This doesn't mean we aren't on a journey of great interest to others. Your internal landscape can be just as rich and revelatory as any exotic trip. A compelling traveler's tale all depends upon your angle of vision and how vividly you, like the shaman-storytellers of indigenous peoples, bring back your story to "the tribe." Being entertained, sustained, and transformed by our travels—both inner and outer—is one distinct advantage that travel memoirs have over other life stories. When you shift your setting, it's sometimes easier to shift your perspective. It's a double vision that can delight the reader.

Think of your inner life as a travel companion to the actual adventure. Keep field notes that are both introspective and observant of every detail around you. The way an artist carries a sketch pad, always have your notebook or recording app at hand so you can write quick character sketches, record insights, and document local color or facts. For example, when Brenda was on a boat in the Florida Keys with several other writers—many of them memoirists—the tour guide casually commented, "The ibis bird was blown here from Africa in a hurricane." Instinctively, every writer on board that boat grabbed a notebook to record this field note. Later that ibis would appear in several memoirs.

Whether you're on a wild adventure, like *Outside* magazine founding editor Tim Cahill, whose memoir *Jaguars Ripped My Flesh* will have any armchair traveler falling out of his chair laughing; or on a spiritual pilgrimage, like Pico Iyer in his nuanced *The Lady and the Monk: Four Seasons in Kyoto* and Jessica Maxwell in her rollicking *Roll Around Heaven: An All-True Accidental Spiritual Adventure*—make your travel memoir as experiential and vivid as possible. If you always remember that your most intimate travel companion is your reader, you'll never lose your way.

PUBLISHING TIPS

When we look at famous-journey memoirs, we can see what they all have in common. We might be dazzled by the exotic locales— Paris, Bali, Italy, the English/Scottish/Welsh moors, the Silk Road, Patagonia—in a word, the world. But when we take a deeper look into the heart and the guts of the book, we find a compelling story.

If the story and inner journey are not there, even if you really write well, what you've got at best is a good magazine article or great travel advertising copy. Sarah Jane notes that while her office is often inundated with travel memoirs, they too often use travel only as background, as color and flavor; and the traveler is only anecdotal, not a character who is developing and changing right before us on the page. Again, beneath the travelogue, there must always be a real story, because without it, what you have is travel journaling, which might be satisfying to you and your friends but isn't yet a book. Just because you're in an exotic locale doesn't make you more interesting to the reader. Sarah Jane has turned down countless manuscripts by writers who didn't understand this concept—as have many editors.

Yet travel writing is actually one of the easiest ways to first get published, and publication of a short piece in an anthology, newspaper, or magazine will help a book publisher take your writing more seriously. Travelers' Tales (see Chapter Notes, page 253, for web link) publishes many theme-centered books, such as *Sand in My Bra and Other Misadventures: Funny Women Write from the Road* and *Women in the Wild: True Stories of Adventure and Connection.* Airline magazines and travel magazines, like *Outside* and *National Geographic Traveler,* are always looking for unique adventure travel stories. These may be less interested in the inner journey, focusing more on "if you go" and travel tips. But they might help you earn some income while writing the deeper, more memoirish pieces about those same trips.

The *New York Times* publishes travel essays almost every week. Brenda's "Hobos at Heart," about railroading and the "steel in the blood" of her family, made it into the *Times* early in her career. A friend of Brenda's who hiked in the Himalayas published her first travel essay *ever* in the *New York Times* at the age of seventy-five.

So here's the recipe for a good travel memoir: Take interesting (even harrowing) trips, voyages, and journeys. Add an inner journey and a compelling story. And mix well. Traveling is a lot like writing. All your outlines and earnest plans may change, but instead, you may discover unexpected and hidden territories within yourself.

Exercise: Always Keep a Travel Journal

At a certain level, every life (or segment of life) can be seen as a journey of sorts. And the payoff for journaling about it, even if your trip rambles and takes many detours, is that it can provide a terrific built-in structure for your book. For example, each chapter can be a different trip or country you visited. There are many excellent books on how to keep a travel journal. One notable book, *Writing Away: A Creative Guide to Awakening the Journal-Writing Traveler*, by Sarah Jane's client Lavinia Spalding, explains that journal-writing is more than just a tool for preserving memories; it is also a means of connecting more deeply with one's inner and outer landscape.

WHAT TO BRING

We love Moleskine notebooks, used by Picasso and many veteran travelers. But also remember your high-tech tools like audio apps, iPads, and other tablets. When Brenda and Linda Hogan, her coauthor for *Sightings: The Gray Whales' Mysterious Journey*, were following the gray whale along the migration path from Mexico to Alaska, they used plenty of waterproof notebooks. So find your unique style of travel and writing, but be forewarned, as Bruce Chatwin wrote in *The Songlines*: "To lose a passport was the least of one's worries: to lose a notebook was a catastrophe."

QUESTIONS TO PONDER WHILE TRAVELING

- How is your journey mirrored in your inner life?
- How is this new place like or unlike your home or your normal routine?
- What triggered or provoked this journey?
- Did your mother or father travel? Your family? How did this shape your worldview?
- Would you have come to this epiphany without travel?
- How did your travels make you see your own life differently?
- What are you escaping? What are you hoping to find?
- What in the culture, terrain, politics, or challenges of this journey has inspired the most excitement and reflection?
- How are you different when you're not in your own home? More open? More romantic? More curious?
- Are you keeping your letters or blogs and taking photos of your travels? Can you use them to inspire chapters of your travel memoir?
- Are you a planner or a spontaneous traveler? How does this reveal your inner life and worldview?
- If there is one place you'd always like to travel before you die, what is it? Why do you want to go there?
- What do you pack in your carry-on, and what does that tell you about yourself?
- Do you like to travel alone or in company? Why?
- What do you always take with you when you leave home? Your laptop, tablet, or cell phone? Your Day-Timer? Your dog?
- If you cannot physically travel, what inner journeys do you take? You don't have to travel far to write a travel memoir. It could be travels around your neighborhood, your city, your local park, or your college campus.

Writing Prompts

In _____, I suddenly became a different person. I traveled
to _____.

If I hadn't traveled to _____, I would never have known
_____.

My time in _____ taught me that _____.

The trip to _____ changed me forever. I _____.

When I travel, I always worry that _____.

It's not until I get on the plane that I feel _____.

I hate to travel, and here's why: _____.

9.

THE MUSIC OF MEMOIR: FINDING YOUR OWN VOICE

I have lived a life with a soundtrack.

~RENÉE FLEMING, *THE INNER VOICE*

Many times in the writing of her memoir *I Want to Be Left Behind*, when Brenda got lost, music found her. Often she'd wonder, "How would I write this scene if it were music?" Suddenly she'd better intuit how to craft the movement of the story—from prelude to chorus to coda. Sarah Jane first suggested to Brenda that she employ hymns from her Southern Baptist childhood as chapter titles. It was a pivotal moment in organizing the book, and it invited an emotional resonance from readers. Many readers have told Brenda, "I know all those songs. I could *hear* your book!"

Music added a sensory dimension to Brenda's memoir, a connection to a larger audience, and a practical way to structure the story. In the chapter "Shall We Gather at the River?" Brenda is inconsolable after committing what she believes is the greatest sin of her childhood. Listen to the cadence of the sentences and how a song enlivens the action and epiphany:

> Now on the muddy riverbank as a procession of penitents paraded past us to the very edge of the Current River, Jessie [my beloved grandmother] began a rousing chorus of "Shall We Gather at the River?"
>
> > *Yes, we'll gather at the river,*
> > *The beautiful, the beautiful river.*
>
> I could see the world more clearly now. The stream of believers floated into the river, their pale gowns flowing up around them like the flotsam of their sins, while they fell trustingly backward into the currents, embraced by the preacher. A miracle happened right then and there—I forgot my own misery.

Forgetting one's own misery is often a must in any memoir—and music can help. Misery may love company, but readers have a short attention span for the one-note samba of "I got hurt, I got hurt, I got hurt" as the main refrain. Story, like music, is never static; it swells and ebbs. It calls for *pianissimo* or *forte*, *largo* or *vivace*, so that the song has a heartbeat, intensity, and forward movement. As in music, emotion is the muscle that drives the drama. A life story thrives on engaging, sometimes surprising, shifts in tone, on the narrator's change, growth, and—most of all—understanding. Remember that the plot of any memoir is the evolution of the narrator over time. Events are the story's song; the strong beat of time is the rhythm. If you think of your life as a musical composition with ever-changing dynamics of sound and sense, you will bring the powerful life force of music into your storytelling.

The five senses are the writer's special effects.

Our very first storytellers were singers of tales. They used rhythmic oral formulas to remember the long incantatory poems they performed. Music is primal and provocative; it is hardwired into our evolution.

LOOK AND *LISTEN!*

Hearing is so powerful—and yet it's often undeveloped, both in our lives and in our writing. Most people's primary or default sense is visual. So our stories are often limited to visual descriptions. Engaging *all* your senses when writing is one of the most important elements we teach in our "Life Story" seminars. After all, the senses are the writer's special effects.

Sound is so strong a sense that it can also be felt. Place your palm against a stereo speaker, and your hand will vibrate. So will your bones, since they are hollow. Our bodies are physically resonant to the frequencies of sound. This synesthesia of hearing and touch can profoundly affect your readers. The crafted music of rhythm and syntax in your writing can also re-create pleasure, even joy—an echo of the sublime. When you open your ears and listen, when you skillfully summon music in your writing, the effect can be dramatic.

In his book *The World Is Sound*, Europe's foremost jazz producer, Joachim-Ernst Berendt, writes, "To hear is to be!" Berendt explains that the eye is more masculine, the ear, more feminine. He cites American psychologists Robert May and Anneliese Korner, whose study of sex differences in newborns revealed that male babies responded more to visual stimuli while female babies reacted more to sound, and this gender difference holds true throughout adulthood. Berendt reminds us, "The whole world is sound, rhythm, and vibration." So when you're writing a scene, don't simply look—listen!

A memoir is not just a solo; it is an ensemble that includes the close-knit and sometimes dissonant harmonies of other voices. Writing a memoir is like singing in a choir, because even though you may have an individual voice, you are attempting sophisticated harmonies and counterpoints with all other characters in your story. In her memoir *Imperfect Harmony: Finding Happiness Singing with Others*, author Stacy Horn recounts her thirty years singing with the Choral Society of Grace Church in New York City. "In times of sorrow (and celebration)," Horn writes, "there are two other things to believe in: music and each other." Her charming and compelling story of every week, weaving her own voice into the acoustic tapestry of her choir, is an echo of the memoirist's job: we must find an individual voice within the chorus of other characters. Horn compares the close harmonies of choral singing to creating a hologram of sound. "It's like you're vibrating like tuning forks with all the people around you," she says. "You don't want it to end."

New research has revealed something amazing—that when a choir sings together, their hearts beat in unison. Could something similar be true for readers and the rhythm of a writer's words? It would be interesting to do some experiments on the heartbeats of readers as they listen to a story or read aloud. Are we such living tuning forks that we vibrate at the same pitch and pulse of someone's story?

Memoir is written in one first-person voice, but it has many other voices in tight counterpoint and imperfect harmonies. Imperfect, because really it is just the storyteller imagining how others speak and sound. Unless you ask other people to write their own dialogue—and we don't advise this—a memoir is always your recollection of another's tale. Attuning your ear to other characters distinguishes them so they are not just simplistic versions of yourself.

Imagine yourself as a director of a very opinionated—and sometimes even raucous—chorus of characters. We all have internalized many voices. Listen to their points of view. Try to capture the sound of their voices in characterization and dialogue. Just as music thrives with multiple parts, so a memoir is enlivened by the dramatic call-and-response of other voices.

WRITE FOR THE EAR

Always remember your audience is made up of both readers *and* listeners. These days, many people listen to audiobooks instead of reading on the page. A good daily practice is to read your story out loud, first alone, and then to an attentive audience. This is where a critique group or a trained ear can be very helpful. As you read aloud, performing the story and voices, you'll begin to hear rambling, dull, or slow spaces where the story stutters or sags, where the dialogue sounds too "written" or artificial. It can also help to listen to the audiobook version of a memoir you are reading in print. Many memoirists narrate their own books, and if you listen to a passage while looking at the same page in the book, you'll add the extrasensory dimension of acoustics. Stories shimmer with intonations, subtle changes in narrative tone, and startling sorrow or tension. You'll hear how the authors, reliving their own stories, *intended* the scene to sound, not just how you interpret the lines in your head. This is enormously helpful to train your own ear for dialogue and dynamics.

Why not develop your individual voice by fully engaging your musical and acoustic senses when writing? Neuroscientist

Daniel Levitin, author of *This Is Your Brain on Music: The Science of a Human Obsession*, told National Public Radio in a 2013 interview, "Life is so unstructured and disorderly much of the time, but music is highly structured and ordered. And so the structure of the music, while you're in the middle of it, really helps you to make sense of what's going on." Memoirists use structure to make sense of life and personal history. Calling upon the building blocks of another art form, like music, can help you discover your own authentic voice. (See Chapter Notes, page 253, for a web link to this interview on NPR's *Talk of the Nation*.)

As you write, here are some acoustic questions to ask yourself:

- What is the music of the time period I'm writing about?
- Is there one song that evokes this scene or this character in my life?
- If I sang this scene for an audience, how would my voice change?
- Am I singing my story in a group or alone? In sync or solo?
- What is the rhythm of my story? Staccato, slow, upbeat, elegiac?
- If my story has a soundtrack, what would it be? Jazz, rap, classical?
- What is the emotion of the song that's driving my story?
- If you are a singer or musician, what music most moves you?
- Can you replicate that musical style in your own voice?

As you write, listen to many styles of music. It will help you learn to play with your syntax, rhythm, and diction. One of the most common comments Brenda writes in the margins of her student's work is "Vary your sentence structure." Change the flow from the predictable subject-verb-noun. Shake it up. Try luxurious and then rapid-fire sentences. Remember the way music swells and softens. Use clauses to support, not drag down a sentence. Read aloud the children's books that excite a child's ear with singsong rhymes, vivid verbs, and surprising nonsense words. No one can read Dr. Seuss's *The Cat in the Hat* and not feel buoyed and charmed.

Also read poetry. One of the reasons Shakespeare's work is so enduring is that it's written in iambic pentameter: *In sooth / I know / not why / I am / so sad*. It is the exact pulse of the human heartbeat, with the accent on the second beat. Lub-*dub*, lub-*dub*, lub-*dub*, lub-*dub*, lub-*dub*. Pound it out on your chest and hear how it moves body and soul. This is the power of consciously using, not just the words you see, but also the words you hear. Make your memoir so alive for the ear that you create not only your own world, but also your own frequency.

In her radiant memoir, *The Inner Voice: The Making of a Singer*, celebrated soprano Renée Fleming writes: "This is the story of how I found my voice, of how I worked to shape it, and of how, it in turn, shaped me." When you write a memoir, you are not only using all of your skills to shape it, you are also being shaped by the story you tell. In crafting the "autobiography of my voice," Fleming explains, "So many of my memories have music attached to them."

So many of our memories have soundtracks accompanying them. Just as every tree makes a different song when the wind moves through its branches, every memoirist sings a unique story when keenly listening to the music of an inner voice.

PUBLISHING TIPS

Often Sarah Jane must handle rejection letters from editors and translate them to her authors. Sarah Jane always reminds her writers that (as we all do) people in publishing make decisions with their hearts and their guts. Only later do they find practical reasons to justify them. But one common theme of these rejection letters is this: "This author really needs to find her own voice."

As Sarah Jane advises, after you find your own voice, all the rest follows. It's not just a voice that drives everything; it's the *storytelling voice*. That's what most holds the reader's attention and makes a book hard to put down. This is the voice Scheherazade summoned to enchant the king and defy, not just rejection, but also death—for 1,001 nights. Not only was the king delighted with her tales, but so was she. The king becomes fascinated with Scheherazade, the storyteller. Her stories spun a deeply intimate and lifesaving bond. This is what good storytelling does—it binds us to the storyteller, as if our lives depend on it.

It's true that voice comes more instinctively and more naturally to some than to others. But with practice, it's something every writer can develop. How? By listening, reading, reading, and— did we mention?—reading. When Brenda was writer-in-residence at Arizona State University, the favorite class she designed was called "Reading for Writers." All her students apprenticed themselves to master voices—Charles Dickens, William Faulkner, Mark Twain, Virginia Woolf, Rebecca West, and Flannery O'Connor, among others. In one-page "voice exercises," the students exactly imitated the diction, syntax, and style of fine authors. Only by trying on other voices do we discover and refine our own. It's like learning dance steps.

Imagine trying to dance Balanchine's choreography without any practice at the ballet barre. Of course, you'd fall down. Like any wonderful dancer, singer, musician, or actor, before you're able to perform with feeling, you need to have practiced your art so thoroughly that when you're onstage, it's effortless. For the writer, in addition to reading, this might mean taking classes or joining a writing group. You'll begin to hear other voices and realize how to shape your own. Having an audience while you're practicing your craft is invaluable. You'll see and hear when listeners get bored or confused, or when they suddenly lean forward eagerly and engage. An audience for your spoken words and stories is an important part of the feedback loop.

Underlying the quality of voice is authenticity. Sarah Jane defines *authenticity* as "intimate knowledge of your subject," a genuine knowledge born of having deeply lived, felt, and understood an experience. Knowing just a little bit about a subject, then making up the rest, will not fool a savvy reader. Agents and editors can catch this half-baked knowledge every time. It just clunks off the page and rings as untrue. Even seemingly inconsequential things, like grammar or spelling mistakes, can break the spell. But when writing has both a strong, unique voice and an authentic tone, a reader can relax and give over completely to the storytelling. We believe we're in the hands of writers who know what they are doing and where they are going.

When agents or editors reject a memoir, they sometimes can't pinpoint exactly why. But when they accept a book for publication, many editors will credit an extraordinary voice. Crafting and developing your own distinctive and true voice can make an ordinary story sing.

Exercise: Write What You Hear and Love

Imitate the voice and style of good authors. Also try to write what you hear. When Brenda was having a difficult time writing *I Want to Be Left Behind*, Sarah Jane sent her *Eckhart Tolle's Music to Quiet the Mind* and a two-CD set, *Rapture*, with rich opera highlights. After all, the subtitle for Brenda's memoir was *Finding Rapture Here on Earth*, so the music was a reminder.

Exercise: Make a Soundtrack for Your Story

Create a playlist as a soundtrack to your story. Each chapter might have a different soundtrack that helps create the mood, the setting, the time period, or the feeling. Brenda is a serious singer and devoted chorale member. When she was working with her editor, Merloyd Lawrence, Brenda created a playlist of songs from her memoir. Brenda lives in a bubble of music, except when she's writing. Then, music overwhelms the words. But many of Brenda's students and other author friends turn on their stereos or stream music from their computers as they type.

Isaac Marion, YA author of the zombie best seller *Warm Bodies* says in his *Burning Building* blog that sometimes music "provides the emotional groundwork for dreaming up the story." As he wrote the sequel to *Warm Bodies*, he provided a playlist, called "Writing Mix," for his fans to offer "a little window into the world I'm building via the music that's inspiring it." It's a terrific idea to make a playlist as you write and to offer it on your blog after publication so your readers can listen as they enjoy your book. Kind of like a sing-along to your life story.

Writing Prompts

My life has been in the major key of _____ and the minor key of _____.

If my life were an opera or a Broadway musical, it would be _____.

Is my life jazz, classical, R&B, hip-hop, or country?

10.

MY FAMILY AND OTHER ANIMALS

Some people talk to animals. Not many listen though. That's the problem.

~A. A. MILNE, AUTHOR OF *WINNIE-THE-POOH*

Most memoirs—and certainly many of the books we discuss—are focused on the human family. Yet animals are a vital part of many families. In memoir, animals can speak through us—and we also can speak through the animals who share our life stories.

Sarah Jane's client Teresa Rhyne learned lessons in survival from her irresistible beagle, Seamus. Soon after the dog came into her life, Teresa was told he had a tumor. Even with surgery and chemo, Seamus was given less than a year to live. Teresa kept a journal of her dog's treatment and soon realized that, unlike her, Seamus was unaware of his diagnosis. In a letter to Sarah Jane, Teresa explained that Seamus simply kept on living and, with "total doggie aplomb," soundly defeated his cancer.

Two years later, Teresa opened her own law office, fell deeply in love, and learned that she herself had cancer. Undeterred, she continued writing. Teresa was told there was a 30 percent chance her aggressive form of breast cancer would metastasize, but she was oddly confident she'd survive. After all, Seamus did.

Instead of falling into silence and acting like a victim, Teresa decided to tell her story. Her journal grew into an inspiring memoir, *The Dog Lived (and So Will I)* The book hit number one on the *New York Times* best-seller list, and Teresa has just sold her second memoir. Teresa's writing was transformative. Everything she needed to know about cancer and about love she'd learned from her beagle, from her writing, and from examining her life.

Animals can be just as important in revealing our own lives as other humans.

WHEN IN DOUBT, WRITE ABOUT ANIMALS

Sarah Jane always advises authors who are in doubt about what to write: consider your dog, your cat, your horse, or your snakes, and, in the case of Sy Montgomery, her larger-than-life pig, Christopher Hogwood. We asked Sy to share with us how she created the character of Christopher, with whom so many readers have fallen in love:

Animals may be more difficult to portray well as characters than people, but this is not because their personalities are less distinct. The difficulty may lie in the fact that as writers, we need to do two things at once to create a portrait of an animal. We must show our character as a member of his or her species, as well as portray a unique individual. One reason animals are so delightful is that they, in the words of Henry Beston, are not brethren or underlings, but "other nations" living by "senses we have lost or never attained." Christopher Hogwood was wonderful, in part, because he was a pig. But he was also wonderful because he was this particular pig, this special individual. Animals are as individual as people are. To do Christopher Hogwood justice, I had to at once, portray his *pigginess* and his personality.

Luckily for me, Christopher Hogwood was an outsize character: 750 pounds, with a personality larger than life. He was loved by many, as evinced by his slops empire, which stretched far beyond the confines of his pen, our eight acres of land, even our village. And that was one way I could portray a character who couldn't speak (in English) for himself: through the affectionate eyes of others. By showing that people were willing to freeze their garbage for months, causing the ice cream to taste like pancakes, or entrust their young children to the care of a huge hog with sharp tusks, we get to see that Christopher is a pig who is not only fun to be with but also someone who is tender and gentle.

But I found other ways to portray him as well. Actions speak louder than words, and this hog was all about action—except when he was about inaction. When he shot out of his pen at a gallop, full of joyous, exuberant power and energy; when a little hand's touch to his big hairy ears would be enough to make him flop over on his side in porcine bliss; when he would stand on his hind legs, mouth open, lips quivering with excitement as a little girl spooned freezer-burned ice cream into his drooling mouth—all these actions expressed the way Christopher related to those around him, his great love for the comforts and thrills of this life. Whatever Christopher did, whether it was digging a pig-size hole in the lawn with his nose, or enjoying the blissful feel of children petting him, he did with gusto and conviction.

And though Christopher didn't speak in English, he did have quite a voice. "Unh, unh, unh! UNH! UNH! UNH!" can actually be very expressive. I quoted him directly through-out the text. Depending on the circumstances, his grunts were quite meaningful He had special, gentle grunts just for the little girls next door, a manly grunt for Howard, a greeting just for me, and a fabulously excited grunt he gave only to his friend Ray, who weighed 300 pounds (I think this is because Christopher thought Ray knew where the food was). He had a grunt of bliss when he was being caressed and cleaned during Pig Spa, and an utterly different grunt when he felt he was being unduly ignored (say, if you walked by the pen and didn't give him anything to eat or pet him). Like quotes from people, animal utterances can give us glimpses into a character's mind.

MY LIFE AS A DOG

Animals can be just as important in mirroring and revealing our own lives as other humans. In Brenda's popular anthology *Intimate Nature: The Bond Between Women and Animals* (coedited with Linda Hogan and Deena Metzger), one of the most popular poems, "Change of Life," by Judith Collas, concludes: "She never felt she was sleeping with the wrong dog."

Memoirs of our lives with dogs are especially beloved—from John Steinbeck's *Travels with Charley* to Garth Stein's *Racing in the Rain: My Life as a Dog*, which goes so far as to write a memoir from a dog's point of view, to John Grogan's *Marley & Me: Life and Love with the World's Worst Dog*. Grogan was a journalist who had never dared write a book. When he and his wife adopted Marley, "the world's worst dog," he kept a Marley journal and then began writing columns about the reckless antics of their golden Labrador pup. Readers responded appreciatively to his Marley stories. But when he wrote a column in the *Philadelphia Inquirer* after Marley's death, he received eight-hundred e-mails or calls in a day. "That's when I knew I had a bigger story to tell," Grogan said in an interview. One of the reasons Marley is such a beloved character in his memoir is because Grogan reveals his dog's flaws as well as his joys. "Yes, he was an attention-deficit, hyperactive, nutty dog," Grogan explains, "but he had a pure heart and an incredible gift of canine-human empathy." Grogan intuitively understood that he wasn't writing a sentimental *Old Yeller,* but about a dog as modern-day antihero.

ANIMALS AS MAIN CHARACTERS

Some of the best-loved memoirs include animals as main characters. One of the most enduring of these is Gerald Durrell's *My Family and Other Animals* set on the sunny Greek island of Corfu. Gerald could have simply written a memoir about the fascinating characters in his own eccentric British family. When he describes his brother, the novelist Lawrence Durrell, Gerald writes that he was always "curling up with catlike unctuousness." Gerald's lifelong work was as naturalist, conservationist, and zookeeper. The titles of his many inspiring books show how much he equates human and animal life as worthy of our attention: *Birds, Beasts, and Relatives*; *Rosy Is My Relative* (about a man who inherits an elephant); and *A Zoo in My Luggage.*

Gerald Durrell's exuberant stories of animal encounters are as compelling as any family memoir. His animal portraits are both zoologically precise and full of quirky personality. Like any memoirist who never outgrows his love of animals, Durrell began scribbling about them from an early age. Durrell biographer Douglas Botting notes that when Gerald was ten years old, he wrote a charmingly misspelled self-portrait. This quote from Botting's book on Gerald Durrell could be the epigram for all of his life stories: "Right in the Hart of the Africn Jungel a small wite man lives. Now there is one xtrordenry fackt about him that he is the frind of all animals."

ANIMALS AS FIRST PEOPLE

Long before Europeans were making friends with animals, indigenous peoples around the world told creation stories with animals as the First People. Native peoples identified themselves by animal clans. Animals were deities, tricksters, brothers, and sisters. These powerful animals are the progenitors of humans, they believed, and as such, ancestors worthy of our deep regard and reverence. They include the monk seal and sea turtles of Hawaii; the wolf and the raven in the Pacific Northwest; Spider Woman and sacred snakes in the Southwest; the brown bear in the Northeast; and the once-mighty panther clans of the South. These first, and still wild animals also reveal our futures and shared survival as much as any of our own science. Polar bears drowning in the Arctic due to global warming; bumblebees and birds dropping out of the air from pollution and pesticides; dolphins washing ashore on America's East Coast in droves—these are life stories of animals that directly affect and foreshadow our own fates.

Why shouldn't animals always be considered main characters and included as "all our relations" in our life stories? And why shouldn't we feel called upon to speak for the animals as Native writer Paula Underwood does in telling the Oneida tribe's life story, *Who Speaks for Wolf.*

Animals can speak through us to tell both their own and our own life stories. In her *Intimate Nature* essay "First People," Chickasaw novelist and memoirist Linda Hogan tells the story of her wildlife rehab work to restore a wounded golden eagle to the wild—and to also restore herself and her tribal traditions. Hogan imagines the eagle's perspective: "I see what I can only call a look of wonder on his face, his beak slightly open, his eyes alert." Sigrid, Hogan's companion and the caretaker of the Colorado injured-raptor haven, says, "He knows he's home."

Writer and activist Sarah James, a Gwich'in woman from Alaska, is the spokesperson for both her tribe and the caribou. "We put ourselves in a humble position," she says, "no greater than bird or duck or plant. We're as humble as they are." This humble identification with other animals, not just as a mirror of us, but also as fellow creatures with dramas and stories in their own rights, is a hallmark of many memoirs. Examining your life alongside other animals is a key to self-discovery.

ANIMALS AS FAMILY

Brenda's first memoir, *Build Me an Ark: A Life with Animals*, was prompted because she realized that at every turning point in her life, an animal had guided and inspired her. Animals were the truth north of Brenda's first memoir. Identifying with animals, especially wild animals, is how Brenda has often reflected back upon herself. All of Brenda's books include animals as main characters, even her novels. Brenda's family cherishes animals and many of them use animal names, like hawk or dolphin in their e-mail handles. The very first story Brenda ever wrote in third grade was from the point of view of a horse.

In her book *Sister Stories: Taking the Journey Together*, Brenda reaches out beyond the animals in her own family to discover a kinship system that includes the sophisticated and matrilineal society of dolphins. In the chapter "The Sisterhood of Animals" Brenda encounters a nursery pod of wild spinner dolphins during a humpback whale research trip in Hawaii:

Imagine dozens of dolphins speeding by in a blur of silver and gray skin, ultrasound, and curve of fin, streaking past, in one breath, as if in one body. Inside my body their speed and sound registers like a trillion ricochets, tiny vibrations echoing off my ribs, within each lobe of my lungs, and spinning inside my labyrinthine brain like new synapses . . . [The dolphins] kept me in their exact center for what seemed an hour, and it was only then that I understood what it feels like to be fully adopted into the deep, welcoming physical communion of dolphins.

I am pod, I felt, with no sense of my single self. *I belong.*

Sometimes animals answer that vital question for any memoirist: *Where do I belong?* Sometimes animals are the guides or the rewards of our search for self. Many times animals show us the way to self-discovery and survival. Our life stories are richer and often more surprising when we acknowledge that they also belong to a kinship system greater than ourselves, that we are interdependent upon the animal kin who guide and abide with us.

When you create real, flawed, and fascinating characters of animals, when they embody a larger lesson or theme, when you avoid easy sentimentality and show how animals evolve or falter alongside us, you can engage many readers. By reuniting with animals in our life stories, we align ourselves with even more ancient traditions of all our early ancestors—those hominids, who beautifully depicted the majestic animals still alive on cave walls. So if you grow weary of first-person storytelling, remember the First People.

PUBLISHING TIPS

Sarah Jane is often surprised by how passionate editors are about animals and the natural world. If you are able to write it well—with humor, keen observation, and without sentimentality—there can definitely be advantages to writing about your life shared with an animal. Whether that animal is a metaphor for a greater truth or an actual pet who lives with you, many emotions that are difficult to access can be more easily expressed from the perspective of a beloved dog, cat, bird, or even the elusive presence of a wild animal.

Children's book editors are used to animal characters being the voices of wisdom, who teach life lessons to their young readers. Publishers have learned that the same can be said for adults. And judging from the success of books like this, it's also good business. Memoirs with and about animals have always been among the most successful and memorable books published.

Exercise: Animal Sketches

Write a sketch about the first time you felt fur or adopted a pet or encountered a wild animal.

Create a character of the animal who has most influenced your life story.

How does the story of that animal parallel or inform your own?

What lessons have animals taught you?

Was your first experience with death with a pet? Tell that story.

Are you a naturalist, rancher, or researcher? Do you work with wildlife rehab, or foster any animals? Write about your experience.

Writing Prompts

If I were an animal, I would _____.

My life changed the moment a dog [or cat, or frog, or other animal] took up residence with me. Tell the story.

An animal saved my life and I saved that animal's life. Tell the story.

In my family, animals were _____.

If there are no animals allowed in heaven, then I _____.

If I were a wild animal, it would be _____.

I most belong to the animal clan of _____.

My totemic animal is _____.

When a/an [animal] looks at my life, he or she sees _____.

11.
SPIRITUAL MEMOIRS

In certain ways writing is a form of prayer.
~DENISE LEVERTOV

All exploration of self is a spiritual undertaking. To write a memoir is to travel a path whose destination is unknown. You summon the courage to look deeply into yourself and are willing to be surprised by what you find there. You think you know who you are. But once you embark on this quest, you might be surprised to discover that what you know is only a fraction of the truth.

PILGRIMAGE

Writing a memoir is actually embarking on a pilgrimage, whether you physically leave home or not. It is a pilgrimage into your past, back to your roots, and into the deep recesses of your heart. What you remember about the things and people you find along the way are like relics, which become powerful reminders for the present. In this process of journeying, you become your own shaman. You enchant yourself and bring your story back to share with readers.

That's what author Mary Swander did in her spiritual memoir, *The Desert Pilgrim: En Route to Mysticism and Miracles*. In searching for a way to reconcile the strict, patriarchal Catholicism of her childhood with her adult doubt and mystical nature, Swander journeyed to New Mexico after a car accident in Iowa left her with a terrible spine injury. There she encountered a Russian Orthodox monk and a Hispanic herbalist who renewed her faith and helped her heal herself. Writing her spiritual memoir changed Swander body and soul.

Sometimes, as with Mani Feniger in her memoir *The Woman in the Photograph: The Search for My Mother's Past*, the pilgrimage is ancestral. Cleaning out their mother's closet shortly after she died, Mani's brother found a photograph tucked away in a dusty envelope. Taken in Germany in the early 1930s it was a remarkable picture of two beautiful young women. Mani writes in her memoir, "I was stunned by the image of my mother, Alice, in a white evening gown . . . Everything about her is graceful—her carefully shaped eyebrow, the playful curl of her hair against her cheek, her painted lips just on the verge of a smile, and the sparkle of gemstones that circle her throat." The woman in this photograph was not the stern, practical, and anxious woman with whom Mani had grown up.

In her eloquent account of her transformative journey into the heart of her mother's hidden past, Mani takes the reader along on her twenty-year search across continents and lifetimes, to uncover a family history that would change her understanding of her mother, herself, and her role in the generational legacy. When Sarah Jane interviewed Mani about her memoir, she wrote:

The Woman in the Photograph began with the TV newscast about the fall of the Berlin Wall. I heard the demonstrators shouting in the language of my childhood, also the language of the Nazi soldiers who drove my parents from their home. But instead of the aversion I had always felt toward that painful era of my family history, an unexpected yearning to understand what actually happened was awakened in me that night. Over the next months and years, this compelling call guided me from Berkeley to New York and finally to Leipzig, Germany, to walk in my mother's footsteps. Like a pilgrim, I carried with me an open heart and a sacred stone that I left on the gravestone of the grandparents I never knew.

While this describes the geographic road map, the writing process itself was also a pilgrimage. Never certain where the information I collected would lead, I had to follow the signs, listen to whomever came forward, and delve into what was revealed. Often I had to let go of preconceived notions, or favorite paragraphs filled with dancing metaphors. Sometimes I had to include disturbing discoveries like the account of my grandmother's leap from the bedroom window. The decision to fully open my heart and my mind allowed the narrative writing process to move forward with an inherent rhythm I could not have planned when I started out. *The Woman in the Photograph* is the gift of this journey, a window into the inner and outer landscape of my quest for truth.

FINDING YOUR SPIRITUAL ROOTS

Many of us diverge from the religious training of our childhoods to embark on a spiritual search of our own. Sometimes we return to our ancestors' spiritual inheritance; other times we blaze our own new beliefs. This search always makes for a fascinating story. Are you descended from a long line of renegade Irish Catholic priests who defied the church and married pagan nuns? Are you a lapsed or backslid Southern Baptist who celebrates the Tao Te Ching? Are you a secular Jew who is searching for spiritual connection by studying both Buddhism and the Kabbalah?

Adding a spiritual dimension to any memoir enriches it, because what we believe suffuses every scene. It is what Brenda calls our "angle of vision" or the lens through which we re-create the world for others and ourselves. Because of her dogmatic Southern Baptist relatives and ancestral line of true believers, Brenda fled the family fervor for a more mystical path. She found it in nature and the ancient wisdom of Taoism, which is nonevangelical and has no church, except the earth. The humor in Taoism and a nonpersonal Divine was balm for her after a childhood of brimstone, blame, and banishing all other believers who did not follow the "one way." Even to this day, Brenda is uncomfortable in any group in which everyone has the same beliefs. "Whether at a football game, political rally, or religious gathering, I always look for the red Exit signs," she writes in *I Want to Be Left Behind*.

Brenda had no intention of ever writing a spiritual memoir; she even resisted it when suggested by editors and Sarah Jane. But one weekend, she gave herself her favorite exercise, "One Scene That Explains Your Whole Life." Suddenly fifty pages poured out, chronicling Brenda's spiritual roots. And like the biblical Daniel, she saw the "writing on the wall." Writing a spiritual memoir seemed the only way to continue to make sense of her life. A scene when she was twelve particularly galvanized her into committing to the spiritual memoir:

Southern Baptist Sword Drills are like spelling bees for true believers.

The Holy Bible was my sword, scripture memorization was the drill, and manual dexterity made the winner. It was a dance of rote memory and fast fingers shuffling through the onionskin pages of the Holy Scripture . . . I was torn between my ambition to win and my growing fear that I was turning into a kind of spiritual automaton . . . I knew scripture. I knew what my parents and everyone around me in this southern hamlet believed, but not what I believed.

Finding out what you truly believe is a profound motivation for writing a spiritual memoir. One of the best ways to nourish a spiritual memoir is to read those of others engaged in their own soul-work. Every year, Penguin Books publishes a collection called *The Best Spiritual Writing*. We use these anthologies in our teaching, especially the 2011 edition edited by Philip Zaleski. Another anthology we admire is *Bearing the Mystery*. Collected from *Image* magazine, it includes many diverse voices and epiphanies. We particularly like Ann Patchett's essay "The Language of Faith," with its conclusion: "Without faith, I would never be able to find the end of the story."

Writing a memoir is embarking on a pilgrimage—whether you leave home or not.

YOUR SPIRITUAL QUEST

Finding the story is the work of any spiritual memoir. The story documents your journey in search of the Divine. It is about your personal encounters on the spiritual and sometimes, specifically, religious path. This experience transforms you, and you share the joy of your discovery with the reader.

Clearly, spiritual quests are universal and without religious, political, gender, racial, or cultural boundaries; one can find wisdom and inspiration equally in Hindu, Buddhist, Christian, Muslim, and Jewish teachings. But please understand: you might well have had an initial spiritual experience, but unless it is followed by a deep inner quest, it is not the basis for a spiritual memoir. In fact, a good spiritual memoir is less about ecstasy and more about slogging; it is hard, painful work.

From Mani Feniger's description of *The Woman in the Photograph,* one can see how many years it took for her to uncover the truth—to know the full story behind the picture. To write her memoir, Mani had to put her whole life on the line. As did Karen Armstrong in her two extraordinary memoirs, *Through the Narrow Gate,* an account of the seven years she spent as a nun; and *The Spiral Staircase: My Climb Out of Darkness,* in which she writes about her more ecstatic and deeper spiritual awakening after having left the convent. As a young English girl of seventeen, Armstrong was filled with religious conviction. But over time, she began to feel that her connection to God was more mystical than conservative, and she found convent life painfully restrictive. Armstrong left the order in 1969 and realized a truer and more profound spiritual awakening. Her books are best sellers, which shows that spiritual memoirs, far from being ancient tomes by theologians, can be very popular.

WRITING AS SPIRITUAL PRACTICE

Many writers see their work as a spiritual path. When *Booklist* critic Donna Seaman interviewed Alice Walker, she asked, "Is writing a spiritual practice for you?" Walker replied: "Oh, it is. It is totally that. I often say, I approach it as if I'm a priestess."

Writing itself with all of its rituals, pilgrimages, and epiphanies is a kind of sacrament. Some of us even feel that a spiritual memoir is a kind of humble practice that reveals the greater and much more mysterious, such as spiritual teacher Mirabai Starr, Sarah Jane's author who is writing a memoir called *Caravan of No Despair,* forthcoming in the spring of 2015. What initiated it was the 2001 death of her youngest daughter, Jenny, in a car accident, at the age of fourteen. This experience created a connection between profound loss and a longing for God that has become the foundation of her spiritual life. Mirabai is the author of *God of Love: A Guide to the Heart of Judaism, Christianity and Islam* and the editor of the popular Devotions, Prayers, and Living Wisdom series.

Another one of Sarah Jane's authors, Nancy O'Hara, could not have written *Find a Quiet Corner*, or any of her other spiritual memoirs, had she not battled alcoholism and then become a Zen Buddhist practitioner.

Nancy wrote, "My first book, *Find a Quiet Corner*, is a product of all this pain, suffering, and renewal. I wanted to share with others what had worked for me. And one thing I know for sure after all these years is: I can't keep anything unless I give it away."

MORAL DILEMMAS

Along the spiritual path there are often many moral dilemmas that ask of us a decision drawn from our deepest beliefs. For a time, the *Christian Science Monitor*, an internationally respected newspaper that was founded by spiritual leader Mary Baker Eddy and prides itself on rigorous neutrality with an ethical lens, ran a series of columns sometimes called "Moral Dilemmas," about "the conflicts we find ourselves facing in daily life." Brenda assigned her students to write about their own moral dilemmas, and quite a few of them were actually published in the *Monitor*. For some, it was their first publication; for others, it was a prestigious publishing credit. (See Chapter Notes, page 253, for a web link to one of the *Christian Science Monitor*'s "Moral Dilemmas" columns.)

One student, a psychotherapist, wrote about how difficult it is to report suspected child abuse, knowing full well the draconian consequences for the whole family. Another student wrote about uneasily facing her own prejudices when her daughter's best friend invited her to a very troubled lower-class home for a sleepover. Another student stumbled with an easy, "almost accidental click" into her daughter's e-mail and found herself invading the family privacy she had always strictly protected.

Our own characters are dramatically revealed through ethical decisions in our lives. Moral dilemmas ground us in the real world of relationships and our struggle to "do the right thing." If you imagine how you've faced moral dilemmas in your own life story, you'll suddenly have many active scenes from which to build a narrative arc. No matter how small they seem, moral dilemmas invite the reader into sorting through the same quandaries in their own ethical lives. Often it's the simple struggle that is the most compelling. As Vivian Gornick says in *The Situation and the Story: The Art of Personal Narrative*, "What happened to the writer is not what matters; what matters is the larger sense that the writer is able to make of what happened." Engaging honestly with our moral dilemmas adds a larger universality and yet an "everydayness" to our spiritual story.

WRITING WITH THE EYE OF GOD

Sometimes it's not enough just to write from our own idiosyncratic and opinionated viewpoint. Sometimes we need a larger vision and a more generous understanding to look with compassion at our life and the lives of those around us. We call this "writing with the eye of God." But beyond stepping outside of yourself to better portray your character, going to the next step is imagining another's point of view, quite distinct from your own.

As a philosophical and spiritual exercise, imagine that everyone in your memoir is equal to you. Every other character's story is as valid and valuable as your own. You just happen to be telling the story from your point of view. You might be a hero in your own life story but a villain in another's memoir. When Brenda was practicing this exercise, she suddenly realized that to some of her more religious far-right relatives, her liberalism and mutinous mysticism might be frightening—she was a strange, invasive spocies, like kudzu in the South.

Try to intuit others' fears and motivations. Even write some scenes in what you imagine to be another character's point of view. This expansiveness will help you to create real, flawed characters for whom the reader has as much empathy as you do. This equanimity and more spacious pose is a good spiritual practice to keep in mind. An anonymous quote that Sarah Jane loves says "All things observed long enough turn to good."

DON'T GET ON THE TRAIN

One of Brenda's favorite stories about working with Sarah Jane on her spiritual memoir is this: Brenda and Sarah Jane both attended President Obama's 2008 inauguration. It was such a historic event that Brenda wrote a chapter about it for *I Want to Be Left Behind*. It was one of Brenda's favorite chapters, a "little darling." But then the cross-country call came from Sarah Jane.

"Sit down, sweetheart, and listen," Sarah Jane said softly. "You must delete this whole chapter from the book."

Brenda protested. "But it's so funny, and I love it, and its history, and we were there to witness, and—"

With a kind of firm tenderness, Sarah Jane interrupted. "In meditation, sometimes you hear a whistle and a whoosh, and suddenly there's this astonishing train taking you far from your focus. You can hear it, listen to it, and observe that train. But if you get on it, you might suddenly wake up and find yourself at a totally different station. Stay centered and clear. *Don't* get on that train."

"Even if that's the glory train bound for heaven?" Brenda teased.

"Especially *that* train," Sarah Jane concluded with a smile that Brenda could hear even over the phone. "This chapter hopped a freight train going nowhere fast."

Here are a few other suggestions to help you get off that glory train in your own spiritual memoir. Brenda hands out her little "Ten Commandments" at workshops, and writers find them very helpful. It's not because Brenda has mastered these rules. Teachers often teach what they also need to learn:

BRENDA'S TEN RULES OF SPIRITUAL MEMOIR

1) The more metaphysical the scene, the more physical and grounded the description.

2) Seeking (questions) makes a better story than finding (answers).

3) Credit your teachers along the way. And keep your sense of humor about your own beliefs, as well as others.

4) Dramatize turning points in your spiritual evolution.

5) Picaresque vs. tragic narrator? Are you a comic or tragic hero in your soul's search?

6) Find strategies to create the self/spirit through fond detachment.

7) The plot of any memoir is the evolution of the soul and the narrator's self-discovery. Plot is different from "this happened, that happened."

8) Do not persuade the reader of your spiritual path. Engage the reader in your search and growing understanding. No evangelizing, please.

9) Diversity is what makes any ecosystem thrive, so remember that your audience is multifaith and multicultural.

10) Build scene by scene. Arrange thematically or chrono-logically. A lively story or search is better than a conversion experience.

Exercises: What You Believe

1) Write a spiritual autobiography tracking your faith, loss of it, epiph-anies, and revelations.

2) Research your spiritual genealogy by tracking the belief systems of your ancestors through to your own.

3) If you had to teach a course called "This I Believe," what story would you tell? By the way, NPR has a series called just this, so you might check out what others have written and use it as a template. (See Chapter Notes, page 253, for a web link to NPR's *This I Believe.*)

4) Transform your compulsions or obsessions into a pilgrimage. Compulsions (or urges or impulses) are typically mindless; they are very, very powerful, but their power often evades conscious thought. Even if it's simply your need to smoke a cigarette, or to walk in a certain direction around the block, or to go shopping, you don't think about compulsions or obsessions—they just *are*. See what happens when you transform them into a spiritual search.

When you do this, your perspective immediately changes and you observe things you hadn't previously noticed. Pay attention as this happens and take notes. Your thoughts and insights will enrich the experience and might find their way into your spiritual memoir. It's also possible that experiencing your compulsions or obsessions this way changes the very nature of them. When you add consciousness and a new perspective, everyday acts can become sacred.

Writing Prompts

As I child, I was taught to believe _____, but when I grew up, I explored _____.

If there is one thing I've learned from my own spiritual practice, it's _____.

When I'm very still, I know _____.

I converted from _____ to _____ because _____.

Philosophically, I'm often drawn to spiritual practices that offer _____.

The deepest moral dilemma of my life was _____.

On my pilgrimage to _____, I discovered _____.

PUBLISHING TIPS

It might come as something of a shock to learn that Brenda and Sarah Jane have very strict guidelines regarding spiritual stories that emanate so joyously from a sense of love and soulful ecstasy. For both of them, it is particularly important that you not be arrogant and holier-than-thou about your understanding. Never assume that your reader is either more naive or less evolved than you.

Sarah Jane has represented numerous spiritual memoirs. She is dismayed at how often she rejects submissions. It's hard to find the right combination of reverence and irreverence. Be reverent about the teachings, she says, but not about yourself. You're still the same quirky or self-conscious, clumsy, shy, funny, vain person you always were. It's that flawed human being that both agents, editors, and readers are interested in reading about. If you grow as a result of your understanding, also grow in wonder and humility. Be a real person who discovers a sacred truth. Because if a real person evolves, so can we.

"Don't be predictable," Sarah Jane is always telling her authors. "Surprise me." Rather than having a spiritual experience while meditating or sitting on a beach watching rainbows, find the spirituality in feeding the chickens, stirring the soup, sweeping the floor. It's your *search* we want to read about. That's often more interesting than your discovery or realization. And if you credit your spiritual memoir as being "channeled," please also channel a rigorous editor.

Walk a fine line, a razor's edge, but stay on track. Keep in mind the principles of homeostasis, the body's ability to regulate itself to an internal temperature of around 98.6 degrees regardless of whether it's hot or cold outside. The same is true for writers. Even in the midst of religious fervor and the most extreme numinous experiences, the skillful writer remembers to come back to a kind of normalcy and just plain sanity, so as not to lose the reader by floating off into the ether.

12.

THE TRUTH, THE TRUTH, AND NOTHING BUT?

What is truer than truth? The story.

~HASIDIC PROVERB

Memoir is a most intimate bond, and sometimes our characters are not content simply to be created by us. If they are still alive, they can talk back; they pick up the phone upon reading their lives filtered through our writer's imagination and argue with us, disown us, call us to account, and sometimes congratulate or thank us. Unlike the fiction writer, the memoirist may be forced to truly face his or her characters, and this adds another dimension, both to the writing and publishing of a memoir.

Because we draw upon our own unique memories, our life stories may be very different from others in the family, the office, the religion, the town, or even the country we share. A memoirist will not exactly mirror everyone else's perspective, so there is always room for disagreement:

"No, that's not the truth."

"It didn't happen that way. That's not the way *I* remember it."

"You're lying!"

It is hard enough to remember scenes from your life without having the specter of these other critics—whether well meaning or competitive—correcting your angle of vision with their own. We always advise our students and clients *not* to show their memoir, especially as they are first drafting it, to family members or spouses, coworkers, or even some friends. Your evolving memoir needs a good first reader, critique group, editor, or agent. These professionals and writing peers know how to nurture a growing book with honest and constructive criticism. They understand how vulnerable a creation can be in its first stages of life, and how much harm unskilled probing and tampering can cause. There will be a proper time to expose your memoir to other readers who are not writers or publishing professionals—and that should be when you have at least a finished first draft of your book. Only then should you consider involving nonwriters in the process, such as family members or friends.

This is not to say that you can't research, and ask questions of fact of others who shared your life story, or even at some final point show certain sections of your memoir to those you've written about. With a few exceptions, Brenda showed her memoirs to people she portrayed in her life story and asked them for fact-checking, especially scientists in *Build Me an Ark* and some family members in *I Want to Be Left Behind*. As you can imagine, not all of Brenda's relatives were rapturous about this spiritual memoir or found its irreverence about Southern Baptists amusing. So they were certainly not her first readers.

Terry Tempest Williams's recent memoir, *When Women Were Birds: Fifty-Four Variations on Voice*, begins with the acknowledgment that at fifty-four, she was the same age as her mother was when she died. As a Mormon woman, Williams's mother was expected to keep a journal; in fact, it was her sacred duty. She promised her journals to her daughter on the condition they be opened only after her death. But when Williams opened these journals, looking for the truth of her mother's life story, she found that the pages were all blank. *"My Mother's Journals are paper tombstones,"* Williams writes. As memoirist, Williams had to make sense of these blank life pages by calling upon her own imagination and interpretations. It is a painful but luminous book to read, and Williams speculates about how religion and her formidable father might have played a part in her mother's self-imposed silence.

MY TRUTH IS NOT ALWAYS YOURS

Childhood memories are particularly open to interpretation from those who shared these early years with you. In a seminal *New Yorker* article, "But Enough about Me," memoirist Daniel Mendelsohn discusses the history of memoir, and the recent revelations that some memoirs, like James Frey's infamous *A Million Little Pieces*, were vastly fabricated. How does any memoirist stray so far from the facts? We certainly don't pardon Frey, but considering how many memoirs have been published in the last decades, it's a wonder there are not more examples of such "untruths."

One clue to "my truth" and "your truth" is how we remember. Mendelsohn ends his article by telling the story of riding on a plane with his photographer brother, Matt. During a family search to discover what had happened to their mother's family, Polish Jews, during World War II, the brothers had asked Holocaust survivors questions about "the tiniest details of life"—from what they ate to who their teachers were, to how they spent their school holidays. Intent on trying to re-create a completely accurate picture of the past, Mendelsohn decries the "mad ambition and the poignant

Trust that your story is amazing enough
and let the truth of it shine through.

inadequacy of those interviews" and trying to reconstruct any-one's past from memory. Even, it turns out, in his family.

When the Mendelsohn brothers hear a high school choir singing a 1970s pop song, Matt turns to his brother and asks if he remembers that they sang that very song together in choir.

> I looked at him in astonishment. "Choir? You weren't even in the choir," I said to him. I'd been the president of choir, and I knew what I was talking about.
>
> Now it was his turn to be astonished. "Daniel," he said. "I stood next to you on the risers during concerts!"

The fact that one brother is convinced they sang together in high school while the other firmly believes he sang in that choir alone is so typical of how siblings and other family members, who shared the same childhood, don't necessarily share the same memories. More often than not, we each have wildly different versions of our shared past. What is the memoirist's responsibility in telling the truth, the whole truth? What is our responsibility to others who share our story? We say, *Vive la différence!* And be prepared to encounter other people's points of view. (See Chapter Notes, page 253, for a web link to this article.)

One explanation for how different your memories might be from those who shared your life is to consider your sensory skills. During the same childhood road trip, you may remember every detail of Salem, Massachusetts, where you witnessed the place women were persecuted as witches; your brother may only remember the trip to Fenway Park; and your little sister may recall every word screamed between your warring parents. That one road trip has three different points of view. Which is the truth? Children, at least until the explosion of social media and photo or recorder apps, weren't always running around recording conversations and scenes. Much of what we remember is forever lost in the physical world, however much it may shimmer and possess us now. Can we trust our memories as "facts"? And what if others disagree? How do we explain our creative process and answer their protests?

CREATIVE NONFICTION

In her clear-eyed essay "Memoir? Fiction? Where's the Line?" author Mimi Schwartz advises: "Go for the emotional truth, that's what matters." Get the facts as right as possible with doing research, asking questions, and checking original sources. Ask for help to confirm your facts from those who were also there. But if your fact-checking is met with unreasonable demands for edits, or threats or angry arguments from people who won't allow you to tell your truth—they lose the privilege of being part of your writing process. We know of one memoirist who was bullied by his family while writing; several siblings and his father tried to censor and control him, demanding to read and "correct" his memoir before publication; they even threatened lawsuits before and after his book was published. (See Chapter Notes, page 253, for a web link to this essay.)

Obviously, those relatives lost any voice or right to be consulted on facts or any other aspects of the memoir. And after his book was published, some of them shunned the author—which wasn't such a bad thing, considering the toxic family dynamic. We know of another memoirist whose husband threatened to kill her if she ever told her truth of their marriage. In writing her book, she found the courage to leave him—and her memoir became a best seller. Ironically, it was the husband who died, of heart failure. The author is happily on to another book.

Sometimes, the process of creating a memoir actually brings people closer together. When we truly listen to other people's points of view, there is the hope of mutual understanding. Once, after a difficult breakup, two writers sat down in a restaurant and made this bargain: First, one would tell the story of their breakup, without any interruption, and then the other. The ex-couple spent six hours in that restaurant, but at the end, each began to understand the truth of the other's pain and perspective. This exercise is different than therapy, in which a trained professional guides, listens, and, if necessary, referees. This technique of mutual listening and allowing each other to express a unique point of view is not about deciding who is "right." It's about understanding that each person's take on a shared story is also valid and true.

When one of Brenda's classes published a memoir collection, *My Mother's Tattoo and Other Family Memoirs*, Brenda, feeling protective, tried to prepare her students for negative reactions from their families and friends. In fact, the book was received with great pleasure and pride by the very people portrayed as characters in the book. Every public reading was like a love-in, and the book actually ended up being profitable. You never know what the reaction will be when you publish your memoir. So we say, prepare for the worst, and be delighted if you are warmly welcomed.

When it comes to writing from your angle of vision, trust your own lens of memory the most. After all, it's your story, your personal truth. You can always say to someone who strongly disagrees with your life story: "I look forward to *your* book on the subject." One way to signal to the readers that the truth you are telling has been reconstructed is to use a disclaimer in the front matter. For example, "This story is true to the best of my ability and drawn from my memory, journals, and letters." Or, if you want to use humor, take a hint from the wildly successful blogger Jenny Lawson, who states her disclaimer right in the parenthetical subtitle of her memoir, *Let's Pretend This Never Happened (A Mostly True Memoir)*.

Remember Joan Didion's famous maxim: "If you remember it, it's true." But how do you fill in the blanks of your memory—re-creating dialogue from childhood scenes, describing a house you barely remember, or deconstructing a painful illness or divorce? What if much of your childhood is a blank? Repressed? Seemingly inaccessible?

Many of our writers begin their memoirs with a sense that their lives are lost in the mists of denial or pain or the miasma of bad memories. But some part of our brain is always watching, recording, and storing our life stories. When we consciously turn our minds back to those scenes, they often return in vivid detail. If you don't remember, you can always use words like "I don't recall the exact shade of his eyes, but what I do remember is how he never seemed to blink."

There are many other techniques we've gleaned over the years to signal to the reader that your memory is sketchy or that you're using creative license to fill in missing pieces. This is just what author Joyce Wadler did in a recent *New York Times* essay, "To the Best of My Memory, It Was Love." Here are some of the ways she qualifies her memories while also making us trust her as a reliable narrator. Writing about her gorgeous cousin, who could "make old men weep," Wadler says:

I don't remember men literally weeping, by the way—that's hyperbole.

And if I did I wouldn't trust myself, because according to an article I read recently, what we consider a memory is actually a memory of a memory, which we refine every time we tell it. And as writers are known to be great embellishers and we are dealing with a story that is well over 55 years old, consider yourself forewarned.

After all of this hedging, Wadler then assures the reader of an essential truth from her direct experience: "But I can tell you with absolute certainty that my cousin Rachel . . . was an actual beauty queen." She then narrates the story the family tells of Rachel's romantic breakup with the bad boy they call James Dean. But years later, when the cousins grow up, Wadler learns the real reason the romance failed—and it's not the "truth" everyone assumed. It was actually Rachel's fault, not James Dean's. Concluding her personal essay with the evidence directly from Cousin Rachel, Wadler admits, "I like my version better . . . Some things are better left unknown."

If you, like Wadler, tell your life story to the best of your memory and still find that some scenes remain inaccessible, just let the reader know you are filling in the blanks. One of Brenda's students had difficulty remembering an adolescence that seemed "ungraspable" because of drug use: "That painful time of drugs and addiction is lost to me forever," he wrote. "But I can call it back and imagine it fully, with the help of magazines and my stoned letters, and films of the Sixties: an acid flashback when I almost threw myself down an elevator shaft; sex with a dazed parade of patchouli-soaked women whose scent lingered days after they left. I can tell this truth: I was lost then—and still am." This technique helps to fill in the missing details of a factually accurate life story set in the turbulent American sixties, a time that is collectively familiar to many of us. So the reader can also fill in some of the blanks.

You can admit faulty memory, but then you can follow that qualifier with a strong claim for what is known. Lee Gutkind, author of *Keep It Real: Everything You Need to Know about Researching and Writing Creative Nonfiction*, explains that creative nonfiction "presents or treats information using the tools of the fiction writer while maintaining allegiance to fact." For examples, we recommend reading Gutkind's *Creative Nonfiction* magazine, one of the best places to find quality nonfiction and memoir.

Another fabulous resource is Robert Root and Michael Steinberg's anthology, *The Fourth Genre: Contemporary Writers of/on Creative Nonfiction*. Brenda has long taught this book in her classes. It covers the landscape of some of the best memoirists at work today. In the wonderful essay "Memory and Imagination," well-known memoirist Patricia Hampl writes about a simple piano lesson from her past that she narrates in exact detail, only to later question her own reliability. "But the truth is," Hampl says, "I don't remember the woman at all. She's a sneeze in the sun and a finger touching middle C. That, at least, is steady and clear." In a frank discourse on the vagaries of memory, Hampl concludes, "memory itself is not a warehouse of finished stories, not a static gallery of framed pictures . . . I write in order to find out what I know."

HE SAID, SHE SAID: WRITING AUTHENTIC DIALOGUE

Writing down remembered conversations is one of the most engaging techniques for a lively memoir. Pick up a memoir in any bookstore and glance at the pages. Are there endless blocks of long paragraphs unbroken by any dialogue? Visually, a book like that promises to be a long slog of "telling" and not "showing." Editors use this criticism to dismiss many memoirs that are simply a passive retelling without the life force of any narrative technique, including active scenes and dialogue. In working with and teaching memoir, we've noticed that the biggest sin of omission in many unpublished memoirs is the lack of realistic and exciting dialogue. Many beginning writers are wary of dialogue, because they aren't comfortable "putting words into other people's mouths" or they don't really remember what the other people in the story said.

"How can I write dialogue I barely remember? Or when I wasn't there to actually hear it?" many students ask. "What about conversations before I was even born? Do I just . . . well, make it all up?"

The answer is, you re-create it. This so-called "embellished dialogue" is acceptable in memoir because the reader understands that the writer is not a voice recorder app. As memoirists, we are recalling *to the best of our ability* what was said. You can always remind the reader that you are writing conversations as you remember or imagine them. We all realize that memory is faulty and that different people may remember completely different snatches of conversation, depending upon their own points of view.

Lively dialogue is vital to a life story. Reconstruct dialogue with a true ear for the sound, diction, accent, and idioms of each person's speech. Just as someone on the page shouldn't act "out of character," he or she must speak in a way that identifies unique speech patterns and beliefs. For example, a very religious character would probably never curse in a conversation; an immigrant's dialogue would have the cadence of her country, and she may even misuse the tricky slang of her new language. If at all possible, ask the person whose dialogue you're recalling to read it over for authenticity. If that's not possible, do your best to tell the truth of the conversation. It's worth the risk of someone protesting,

"That's *not* what I said!" because dialogue is a vital element of storytelling and it's important to include dialogue in every scene.

With only endless description or passive interior, scenes can sag and grow tiresome. Conversation on the page is very different than what you hear at your local Starbucks. Why? Because writers are not reporters; we are storytellers. We know how to condense, intensify, and focus a dialogue between characters in such a way that the reader "hears it."

If you were to record one of your conversations and then try to replicate it word by word for your memoir, you'd soon discover that the ear is very discerning and impatient. It immediately recognizes dialogue that is information-giving and not really "spoken." A line like "Didn't you tell her that I was a bartender in that Vegas brothel in 1989, before we got hitched?" is obviously more about giving the reader backstory than a real conversational exchange.

Crafting authentic dialogue is also a technique for suggesting other points of view than the narrator's. It is a release from what can too often feel like being trapped in an elevator with a first-person narrator. Dialogue opens up the action to other voices and tones. Dialogue is the muscle that moves scenes and story along.

Exercise: Subtext Game

Brenda plays a subtext game with her students that you could try with your writers' group. Set up two rows of chairs. In the first row are those characters reading only the dialogue as written on the page. Standing behind each speaker is a second row, speaking the imagined subtext—or what is really in the minds of the characters. And behind both rows of dialogue and subtext stands the narrator, who comments on it all.

Here's a simplified example of this very lively game.

First Row: Dialogue

SID: Wow, is it really *you*, after all these years?

MARIAN: Oh, Sid, you haven't changed since high school!

Second Row: Subtext

SID: God, not her again! The one person I never wanted to run into at this reunion. Did we really sleep together on prom night? She's really blobbed out! How can I get away?

MARIAN: He has no bloody idea that he got me pregnant. Clueless! Why did I come? Did I seriously think he'd change? Should I ever tell my daughter who her father really is?

MATURE NARRATOR: It had seemed like a good idea to at least try to make contact with the man who had fathered my only child. But now when I saw who Sid had become—the droop of his belly, the same self-satisfied grin that back in high school signaled confidence and now just seemed silly and unearned—I realized that sometimes love is better lost and left far behind.

So much can happen in subtext, especially if it contradicts the spoken dialogue.

Another great exercise is the Eavesdropping Game. Go with a fellow writer to a coffee shop. Bring your laptops. Sit as if engrossed in your own work, but transcribe exactly the dialogue you hear from a nearby table. You'll discover upon reading your dialogues to each other that you each censored, filtered, and changed what you heard. This exercise perfectly exemplifies the law of physics: when we observe something, we change it. Dialogue needs to be transformed and well crafted to sound authentic on the page. It will dramatize and energize your life story more than almost any other technique you can imagine.

This is the art of a true memoir: employing these essential narrative techniques, filling in the blanks of memory, and using creative nonfiction to make your story come alive on the page. As the Nobel Prize–winning author, Toni Morrison, writes in the essay "The Site of Memory," "the crucial distinction for me is not the difference between fact and fiction, but the distinction between fact and truth. Because facts can exist without human intelligence, but truth cannot."

PUBLISHING TIPS

One of Sarah Jane's favorite editors is Toinette Lippe, who worked for many years at Alfred A. Knopf and signed well-loved authors, including Stephen Levine, Gunilla Norris, and Ram Dass. Toinette is herself the author of two memoirs, including *Nothing Left Over* and *Caught in the Act*. Here's what Toinette has to say about writing the truth:

In the early 1960s, Nicolas Bentley, one of the founding editors of the British publisher André Deutsch (where I worked at the time), wrote a memoir entitled *A Version of the Truth*. Its title has remained with me all these years. Bentley didn't claim to have the truth, the whole truth, and nothing but the truth. No one can make that claim—even though many do. Everyone's experience is different, even if, say, three people are present in the room. They are not standing in the same place and all that is already in their minds is the backdrop for what is happening, so that each will describe different aspects of the event and, perhaps, reach a different conclusion about what took place.

Sarah Jane believes that publishing is still an enclave of civility that, more often than not, exists within a culture of trust. In a culture of accepted, even admired, dog-eat-dog manipulation and tricky business dealings, the *niceness* of publishing seems surprisingly old-fashioned and refreshing, almost Victorian. Not that publishing has been spared fallout from the digital age, globalization, the rise of the accountants, and corporate takeovers—but deals are still made (and honored) on the basis of a handshake. Never, for instance, has Sarah Jane ever had a publisher renege on a contract.

Editors do truly care about authors and their books; they are invariably intelligent, dedicated, and hardworking. The last thing an author would ever want to do, even unwittingly, is to deceive one by submitting a manuscript based on information that wasn't true. Often, in the process of writing, we realize a truth not previously obvious to us. A kind of poetic reality is revealed. And this is fine, sometimes even magical. But what obviously isn't fine is fabrication: willfully falsifying the truth to make a memoir sound more interesting.

What's required is a sensible kind of honesty, just what's true enough. It isn't a problem if some minor descriptive details change or unimportant conversations aren't exact. And if something actually happened on a Tuesday and in your story it happens on a Wednesday, so what? (Unless, of course, the Tuesday was September 11, 2001—then it would matter very, very much.) In your memoir, try to be as truthful and reliable as possible. Your reader counts on you to be so. Trust that your story is amazing enough and let the truth of it shine through.

Exercise: Discovering Your Truth

On a large piece of paper draw four columns:

1) What I Knew Then

2) What I Know Now

3) What I Don't Know

4) What an Omniscient Narrator (Hidden Observer) Knows

Fill in each column about a certain memory or event in your life story and compare them. We promise you'll be surprised at how much will come back to you, which will allow you to fill in even some of the deepest blanks.

Writing Prompts

Everyone tells a different story about that event, but mine is

_____.

I'll admit, the facts are foggy, but the emotional truth is _____.

When I revisit that scene, every detail is etched in my mind: the

_____, _____, and _____.

No one in the family knows or remembers this: _____.

13.

"FOODOIRS" AND FEEDING THE HUNGRY WRITER

---

*Yet again I had recalled the taste of a bit of madeleine
dunked in a linden-flower tea which my aunt used to give
me (although I did not yet know and must long await the
discovery of why this memory made me so happy) . . .*

~MARCEL PROUST, *IN SEARCH OF LOST TIME*

Marcel Proust's words are perhaps the best-known quote about
food and memory ever written. Everyone eats. So memoirs about
food—its culture, its preparation, and its pleasures—always make
engaging stories. Food also carries cultural and familial backgrounds that add fragrant and tasty details to your storytelling.
Here are Brenda's first lines of her own tribute to Marcel Proust—
and her mother's fabulous Southern cooking—from *Lost* magazine,
"A la Recherche du Cheese Perdu." (See Chapter Notes, page 253,
for a web link to this story.)

Pimento Cheese sandwiches are. the petite Madeleines of my
childhood.

My mother is a splendid Southern cook who taught herself "from scratch." The first time she made chocolate chip cookies as a girl, she proudly mixed the sticky batter and then deposited a thick mound of chocolate-studded dough onto a cookie sheet. She watched through her General Electric oven's glass window and waited patiently for the little mountain of dough to separate into two-dozen perfect cookies.

Immediately, the cultural character of Brenda's mother is revealed through the Southernness of pimento cheese, and this opening also suggests a fond portrait of her early years as a cook when she so hopefully awaited for cookies to form themselves. This says a lot about the mother's naiveté, but it also reassures readers that she learned to be a remarkable cook. So there is a signal of character evolution that the reader wants to follow. The more unusual or ordinary your story, the more vital the subject of food is. Food keeps it real. Food humanizes us and transcends every barrier. So please, remember to invite your readers to "break bread with you." We think that's awfully good advice.

So what does this have to do with writing? The connection is that the way we approach eating ultimately affects everything else about our character. One of the main ways we create self-portraits and bring to life others on the page is through sharing food. Scenes of family or holiday meals are almost always rich with character development, dialogue, and sensory details that make the drama come alive. At every holiday, Brenda gives her students the assignment to write about a time when all the characters were gathered together to eat. These scenes are so revealing and compelling that they almost always end up in a student's memoir.

A good place to start your memoir is with something we all do several times a day—eat. Let's face it, writing is a hunger-making business, and that hunger is not just hunger for food. The famed food writer M. F. K. Fisher says: "When I write of hunger, I am really writing about love and the hunger for it, and warmth and the love of it and the hunger for it." Cookbook writers instinctively understand the connection between eating, love, spirituality, and writing. And it's something they've come to ritualize. Memoirists have much to learn from food writers.

SHARING FOOD AND STORIES

Brenda was fortunate to find in her very first editor, Judith Jones at Knopf, a master of good writing, especially about food. After all, Judith discovered Julia Child, James Beard, Chinese chef Irene Kuo, Egyptian cookbook writer Claudia Roden, and the enduring Southern cook Edna Lewis. These and Jones's other food writers revitalized American's relationship to eating and culture to make us truly a melting pot in the kitchen. In her own memoir, *The Tenth Muse: My Life in Food*, Jones generously passes on her food wisdom, especially "at a time when most kitchens seem to be empty." The beginning of her memoir is a lovely example of how food can be a main character in your own life story:

> When my mother was well into her nineties, she announced that she had an important question for me and wanted an honest answer. I steeled myself for something weighty, perhaps about whether I believed in heaven and hell.
>
> Then she looked at me and asked: "Tell me, Judith, do you really like garlic?" I couldn't lie. Yes, I admitted, I adored garlic.

This opening story not only charmingly introduces the main character—a woman who will follow her own refined senses— but also shows us how willing Jones is to defy traditions to follow her own passion for food. This opening story says, in a much more interesting way, *You are what you eat*. Food for Judith Jones is what shapes and defines her character. When you write about food, think of it as a characterizing detail that reveals to the reader who you and others really are. If ever in doubt as to what scene to write—re-create a dinner scene. It gathers characters at a literal table and offers a wonderful opportunity for dialogue and to celebrate tastes and smells.

Jones's very inquisitive and lively focus on food is also how she thematically organizes her memoir; each chapter narrates her developing search for good food. In the chapter "The Pleasure That Lasts the Longest," she tells the story of dining with poet Galway Kinnell, and their conversation about how much cooking is like writing: "You have to find the exact word (or ingredient), to pare down (to get the essence of a flavor), to make seamless transitions (the compatible movement from one course to another)." Of course, the difference between cooking and writing, Jones notes, is that the writer can revise over and over, but the cook must "get dinner on."

Doesn't writing inspire you to go into the kitchen and chop or stir something?

WRITING ABOUT FOOD

The next time you feel blocked, instead of getting up every twenty minutes and looking in the fridge to find something that will prompt you to write that one perfect sentence, maybe you should try, as several cookbook authors suggest, finding your favorite recipe and cooking while brainstorming your book. Here are a few of our favorite quotes to inspire you:

*Writing is 90 percent procrastination: reading
magazines, eating cereal out of the box, watching
infomercials. It's a matter of doing everything you can
to avoid writing, until it is about four in the morning
and you reach the point where you have to write.*

~PAUL RUDNICK, AUTHOR OF *I SHUDDER: AND OTHER
REACTIONS TO LIFE, DEATH, AND NEW JERSEY*

*I find that stirring helps me clear my thoughts,
whenever I feel blocked and confused.*

~AGLAIA KREMEZI, AUTHOR OF *THE MEDITERRANEAN PANTRY*

*Cooking is my way of practicing mindfulness. I write
early in the morning after my meditation session,
before breakfast, but with a cup or two of tea.*

~SU-MEI YU, AUTHOR OF *CRACKING THE COCONUT:
CLASSIC THAI HOME COOKING*

*I go into a different state when I cook. The rhythm of the
chopping knife, the feel of a wooden spoon stirring, the
sound of sauces bubbling away . . . for a moment I'm in
that place Whirling Dervishes must visit as they spin—a
place that's complete and whole, focused and at ease.*

~ELISABETH ADDURU, *A DUCHESS COOKS IN BROOKLYN* BLOG

"I always write hungry. I feel it awakens creativity," says Titti,
Sarah Jane's friend in Naples, Italy, where there is an abundance
of tempting things to eat. On the other hand, Aglaia Kremezi, who
is Greek, suggests that "the hours after a light lunch and a glass of
wine are the perfect time to put thoughts into words."

"I am a hedonist at heart," says Susie Middleton, author of *Fast, Fresh & Green* and *Fresh from the Farm: A Year of Recipes and Stories*, "so I must be comfortable and well-treated to start writing. That means a mug of hot coffee with cream and a bowl of dark chocolate chips at my side. In winter, I need to feel warm, so in our drafty farmhouse, a little electric heater sits at my feet and toasts my toes. My visual surroundings are important, too; I love my little office, which is full of worn old wooden furniture and far too many books, and my desk is a big old pine table surrounded by wooden chairs and a fabulous and surprisingly comfortable ladder-back bench which I spread my papers out on. It's a secure and familiar place."

Doesn't reading this inspire you to go into the kitchen and chop or stir something? And write about it? Here to inspire, reenergize, and cheer you on is one of our favorite recipes. So let's break bread together!

"ENLIGHTENMENT" RICE PUDDING

While in no way are we puritanical about what you (or we) should eat, if your diet consists solely of fat and sugar, we suspect all you will produce is a big yawn. We make one exception to that rule: if someone says, "You look as though you are starving, here's some rice pudding," eat it. Like the kind goatherd girl Sujata did for the Buddha, they might be offering you "enlightenment" rice pudding.

As Buddhists tell it, the Buddha was sitting beneath the bodhi tree meditating whereupon, seeing that he looked starved and emaciated, Sujata prepared and served him a large bowl of rice pudding. The following morning the Buddha was fully enlightened.

Although the Buddha left many teachings on the true nature of existence and how we might open the door to real happiness, neither he nor Sujata left the recipe for that life-affirming dish. So Sarah Jane asked an Indian friend for one. Here's a recipe for *kheer*—which is what rice pudding is called in India. However, we suspect that Sujata used goat's milk, so if you are truly interested in expanding your consciousness—you might have to find some.

Indian Rice Pudding (Kheer)

Makes 6 servings

1 cinnamon stick

3 cardamom seeds, split

4 cups (32 ounces) unsweet-ened coconut milk

½ cup sugar

1 cup basmati rice, soaked in cold water for about 20 min-utes, then drained

½ vanilla bean, split

Pinch of saffron (optional)

4 tablespoons unsalted butter, at room temperature

½ teaspoon rose water (optional)

Crushed pistachios or almond slivers

Using cheesecloth wrapped with kitchen twine, make a satchel with the cinnamon stick and cardamom seeds.

Whisk the coconut milk and sugar until it dissolves.

In a medium-to-large heavy-bottom pot, place the rice, spice satchel, split vanilla bean, saffron, and coconut milk mixture.

Bring to a boil, uncovered, then lower to a very low simmer for 30 minutes. After 30 minutes has passed, gently mix with wooden spoon to make sure the rice isn't sticking. If it is, lower the heat. Check rice for sticking or burning by gently mixing every 10 to 15 minutes. If, after most of the liquid has been absorbed, the rice still isn't cooked, add $\frac{1}{2}$ cup very hot tap water to the pot, mix gently, and cover until the rice is soft.

Once done, turn off the heat, discard the spice satchel and vanilla bean, then gently stir in the butter and rose water, if using, until incorporated.

Serve warm or cooled with the nuts on top.

To all of you hungry writers, bon appétit!

PUBLISHING TIPS

The culinary memoir, often dubbed a "foodoir," was once described by *New York Times* food editor Christine Muhlke as "one part chick lit mixed with one part chicken lit." There are a great many examples of foodoirs, like Lisa Abend's *The Sorcerer's Apprentices*, Gabrielle Hamilton's *Blood, Bones & Butter: The Inadvertent Education of a Reluctant Chef*, Aimee Bender's *The Particular Sadness of Lemon Cake*, and many more. But foodoirs can do a lot more than entertain. While we might not necessarily want to try duplicating every one of Julia Child's recipes in order to revitalize our life or our marriage the way Julie Powell did, we loved reading and fantasizing about it in her *Julie and Julia: 365 Days, 524 Recipes, 1 Tiny Apartment Kitchen*.

Chronicling one's life through the prism of food, however, is not solely the domain of women. Many men have done so too. Star chef, writer, and TV personality Anthony Bourdain did it in his many memoirs, from *Kitchen Confidential* to *Medium Raw*, as did Frank Bruni in *Born Round* and Jeffrey Steingarten in *The Man Who Ate Everything*. And there have also been men who use food for much more serious stories, like Grant Achatz, owner of the Chicago restaurant Alinea.

In 2007, soon after he had been named one of the best new chefs in America, he was diagnosed with Stage IV squamous cell carcinoma (and irony of ironies, the disease was centered in his tongue). His journey is described in *Life, On the Line: A Chef's Story of Chasing Greatness, Facing Death, and Redefining the Way We Eat*, written with coauthor Nick Kokonas. A radical treatment saved Achatz's life but also resulted in his loss of taste. Several months later, however, having rarely missed a day of work, he received the James Beard Foundation's Outstanding Chef Award. His memoir is not only about a love for food—it is also a tale of survival.

Survival is also what's on food writer Paula Wolfert's mind, in her brave and outspoken battle with Alzheimer's disease. On *PBS NewsHour*, she said it's time to boldly confront the disease and bring it out into the open. Aside from speaking out, consulting with doctors, and exercising, Wolfert is combating memory loss with power foods and cooking.

Sarah Jane says that while food can be a metaphor for life and for love, it can also be a manifestation of life itself. If you have an intimate connection with food (delectable romps filled with wonderful memories of sights, smells, and tastes; or, food as a fundamental and essential force in your life), why not interweave it into your life story?

But always remember, every published food memoir—about local kitchens or exotic locales, about home-cooked comfort foods or esoteric recipes, from nostalgic to powerful and life-affirming—have one thing in common. A good story. You can be absolutely sure that you won't see a foodoir on any bookstore shelf or websites without one.

Writing Prompts

I'll never forget one holiday meal with my family when _____.

My family's food traditions are _____.

As a cook, I often equate food with _____.

I am not a confident cook, but that doesn't keep me from loving food. My favorite food stories are _____.

Eating in my family is all about _____.

Every time we get together for supper, we argue about _____.

14.
YOUR LEGACY

Carve your name on hearts, not tombstones.
A legacy is etched into the minds of others
and the stories they share about you.

~SHANNON L. ALDER

A legacy memoir is something you write for posterity, your family, your adult children, your grandchildren, or maybe just for yourself. It's not necessarily written to be published. However, unless this is a personal journal that you plan to have burned when you die, you are still writing to be read—perhaps while you are alive, or not. Even though there isn't an agent or an editor to seduce, you still want your memoir to be more than a simple record or account. You want it to be a meaningful and enjoyable read.

Your memoir might change somewhat depending on who you are writing for, but the following holds true: do not take the details of your early years for granted. Remember to establish the "when" and "where"; remember to place your story in a particular time and in a specific place. In other words, when you were born, where you were born, and what was happening in the world at that time. If your memoir is to be read by preteens or teens, let them know in what ways *your* world was different to the one they now take for granted. You're here now to tell that valuable tale.

YOUR LETTERS AND E-MAILS

You probably have photographs of yourself as a child, growing up, or getting married. The same is true for letters you've stowed away in dusty bins: love letters, Dear John letters, letters apologizing for some long-forgotten slight, pledges of forever friendships. One of Brenda's students, Susan Bloch, has a priceless cache of letters and e-mails from her elder aunt Dolly, whose life traces the shared story of Susan's grandfather. Like many Jews in Lithuania in the 1890s, he fled ruthless conscription into the Red Army for Johannesburg, South Africa. Aunt Dolly should have been a memoirist, because her polished and philosophical writing style is so alive. In conversations with Susan, Aunt Dolly would always ask, "Now that I'm eighty-eight, are we nearer to solving all the mysteries of life, death, soul, and eternity?"

It was Aunt Dolly who ignored South Africa's brutal apartheid policies to socially engage with blacks. Aunt Dolly was an "outlier" who followed her dream and in 1945 courageously moved to the new state of Israel. On her deathbed, she told her niece: "Promise me you'll do what the Talmud says is your God-given duty: 'Live your last day on earth to the fullest.' Just do that for me, because I don't think I can anymore. I'm so tired."

Though Aunt Dolly has passed, her letters live on in her niece's own memoir-in-progress, which, in turn, will inspire the next generation. Here's one of the last e-mails Aunt Dolly wrote the week before she died in Johannesburg:

Do you know Schubert's arpeggio sonata? There are so many pauses during the music and somehow the silence seems to affect one emotionally more than the music. Now, I can't find words to express those wonderful feelings I had when you were here, so multiply the following silence by at least a million more.

If you are hesitant to write an entire book, why not offer a legacy to your next generations by writing a series of letters in which you tell your life stories? If you are fortunate enough to have the actual archival letters, photos, e-mails, and maybe even stories from other family members, include these. Often, writing down these life stories can be more nourishing than financial legacies. They not only give family history, but they also generously offer a perspective of that history by one who actually lived it.

In 2013, the Museum of Jewish Heritage in New York City staged a poignant exhibit of some of the letters Jews in Europe wrote as they attempted to find sponsors in the United States and South America to help them escape the Holocaust. Some of these people managed to come to America, and photographs of entire families who safely relocated were also on display. Do you have anything like this? Please consider gathering them and adding your own story.

What about pictures of weddings, summer vacations, graduations, your first child or first grandchild or great-great-grandchild. Or . . . or . . . or. In addition to the physical details of your story, let your audience know what lessons life has taught that you'd like to pass on. This is where you get to write not only about what you've accomplished, but also insights and inspiration you've gained.

Maya Angelou, in her mesmerizing public talks, always credited her ancestors, who were stolen from their homelands and endured the Middle Passage as slaves bound for America. Angelou believed she "stands on their shoulders" and, in times of her own personal despair, she drew upon their heroism to remembered "how they got over." Many African Americans can trace their genealogies back only as far as slavery. Some, like Alex Haley, whose book *Roots* launched a genealogy boom, imagine the lives of their ancestors to better understand the present. If you think of your memoir as part of a stream of souls before you and to come after you, your personal life story joins the voices of so many others—and it is a gift to the future. You become part of a precious and ever-weaving tapestry.

"HAPPY TO HAVE BEEN HERE"

Oddly, it is sometimes by writing your legacy memoir that you discover exactly who you are and what you believe in. And all the things people will say when you're gone—you get to say them now, while you're alive. That's what Jane Catherine Lotter did. Realizing that she was dying from endometrial cancer that had metastasized to her liver and abdomen, Jane Catherine, a sixty-year-old Seattle author, mother, and wife, known by friends and family for her quick-witted charm and spunk, wrote her own poignant, life-affirming obituary.

A meditator and student of Buddhist philosophy—which she said helped her accept what she couldn't change—Lotter wrote:

At any rate, I am at peace. And on that upbeat note, I take my mortal leave of this rollicking, revolving world—this sun, that moon, that walk around Green Lake, that stroll through the Pike Place Market, the memory of a child's hand in mine.

And she signed off with: "Beautiful day, happy to have been here."

Jane Catherine's self-obituary was published in the *Seattle Times* on July 28, 2013. It created such a stir that it went viral online and was reprinted in newspapers around the country. *New York Times* writer Michael Winerip wrote an article about it, under the title "Dying with Dignity and the Final Word on Her Life." (See Chapter Notes, page 253, for a web link to this article.)

All the things people will say when you're gone—
you get to say them now, while you're alive.

One of the more poignant legacy encounters Sarah Jane has ever had took place in a heated saltwater pool at Gurney's Inn in Montauk, Long Island. Sometime between the end of winter and the beginning of spring, Sarah Jane was recovering from one of those persistent colds that just seem to hang on forever. Believing, as author Isak Dinesen did, that "the cure for anything is salt water—sweat, tears, or the sea," she decided that what she needed, instead of chicken soup, was to immerse her whole body in warm saltwater. As luck would have it, she was giving a workshop in Sag Harbor on the weekend, and about twenty minutes farther east, situated on a cliff overlooking the Atlantic Ocean, was Gurney's Inn, which has a spa with a warm saltwater pool.

Luxuriating in the pool that Sunday afternoon, she was soon joined by a group of three women. Floating in the warm water there, women often share stories. Upon learning that Sarah Jane had driven from New York City to give a memoir-writing workshop, one of the women, Anna, grew very excited. Anna loved to write, and she also worked at a hospice on Long Island.

The first time she offered a hospice patient to write down his life story, it was simply a gesture of kindness; but once she saw the reaction, she decided to make it her mission. It turned out to be the greatest gift for both those who were in hospice and also their families. "Nothing brought my hospice patients a greater sense of peace and closure," Anna said, "than knowing someone had written down a life story. And nothing could be more valuable to their families—many of whom were not familiar with all of it."

Recently, to her surprise, Sarah Jane discovered the now parchment-colored sheets of her own father's life story in an old paper bag wrapped in cheesecloth. Robert Freymann was born in Leipzig, Germany, in the early 1900s. He was a doctor, the son of the son of the son of a doctor, all of whom were brilliant diagnosticians, and Jewish. Robert was charismatic: dark haired, blue-eyed, and drop-dead handsome. The first thing that struck Sarah Jane as she read was page after page of amorous encounters. Indeed, her father adored women and was loved by them in return. But interspersed among accounts of these passions were accounts of his *other* passion—medicine. Sarah Jane read fascinating medical stories as well as details from his amazingly picaresque life. Here's a tiny vignette taken directly from her father's memoir:

March 10, 1933. Berlin. Two months after the Reichstag, a detachment of S A Hitler men stopped in front of the x-ray hut of the U Krauburhaus. One of the men went inside and asked for the Chief Assistant—me. He saluted smartly, raising his hand in the Nazi salute. "Heil Hitler," he said "Congratulations. You will now be Chief of the Department." I asked him why and he answered "Because the current chief is a Jew." "Oh, no" I replied, "The chief is Christian. I am the Jew." The man's face expressed utter astonishment and deep disappointment because he and I had become rather friendly in the past few weeks . . .

Now, if that were your father's story, wouldn't you want to read about what happened next? As another of Sarah Jane's friends, Gianluigi Quentin, who was born in Italy in the 1930s, says about the legacy memoir he wrote for his grandchildren:

In former times, knowledge was passed down from father to son and from grandparents to grandchildren. Today, the focus is so concentrated on the future that there is a disregard for many of the important lessons of the past. This is why it is important that we elders write our memoirs—so that younger generations can learn from our experiences.

THE THIRD AGE

So here is yet another compelling reason to consider writing your legacy memoir—there is something unique about those of us who are sixty or older. We, who have been influenced by the age of the baby boomers, have established new values and forged our own paths, refusing to follow traditional roles and go anywhere quietly. Consider that never before in our history have there been this many Americans over the age of sixty with life expectancies that have increased so dramatically. As Marc Freedman writes in *The Big Shift: Navigating the New Stage Beyond Midlife*, in this "Third Age" is a group of unique adults who refuse to grow old passively and are a still-untapped resource of wisdom and talent.

It is his personal experience of growing old and the lessons learned from wrestling with this new age that Reb Zalman Schachter-Shalomi writes about so creatively and insightfully with his coauthor, Ronald Miller, in *From Age-ing to Sage-ing: A Profound New Vision of Growing Older*. Reb Zalman talks about living into our old age with spirit and a continuing willingness to learn and grow. He urges us to become mentors to a younger generation and models of how to age fearlessly and well. What better way to do this than writing your legacy? Warner Books first published Zalman's book—which Sarah Jane is proud to have represented—in hardcover in 1995. It has been such an inspirational guide, it was reissued this year.

Scientific research shows that the aging brain is actually more creative than the younger brain, another argument for leaving a written legacy of your life story. A 2013 *Time* magazine article, "How to Live Long," notes that with age, the two hemispheres of our brains work more in sync, and so intuitive leaps spark more often than in younger, more rigidly organized brains. The nimble and engaged writer's mind is like an anti-aging drug. Everything we do in writing a memoir stimulates memories, challenges us to recognize patterns, and inspires us to make sense of our lives.

This heavy lifting for the brain keeps it lucid, adaptable, and alive. In fact, the regenerative power of a brain actively at work on writing a life story can actually *increase* longevity. "It's not just the luck of living a long life that allows some people to leave behind such robust bodies of work," the article concludes, "but that the act of doing creative work is what helps add those extra years." Sometimes only age can give us the free time, attention span, perspective, and security to really contemplate our lives and share our stories. (See Chapter Notes, page 253, for a web link to this article.)

About a week before her birthday, Sarah Jane attended a silent meditation retreat on "wisdom in aging" near Manhattan with the Tibetan Buddhist teacher Tsoknyi Rinpoche. The participants, who ranged in age from their midfifties to mideighties, were the kind of sage and engaged elders that both Reb Zalman Schachter-Shalomi and Marc Freedman write about.

The first meditation session was at 6:15 a.m., and almost everybody attended. While some sat on chairs, many sat cross-legged on cushions on the floor. This was a group of serious meditators; they asked intelligent questions, laughed frequently and easily, and were not afraid to question the teacher about dying. Some had driven relatively long distances to attend, and although several were retired, there were also those who worked lovingly and fearlessly with the dying in hospices, while others were lawyers, psychotherapists, and educators.

Once the participants were no longer required to keep silence, Sarah Jane was free to speak with several of them. One of them was Rosalie, who founded her own school in Saratoga Springs, New York, called The Beagle School Preschool (named after Charles Darwin's ship and voyage of discovery). Rosalie told Sarah Jane this story about an unusual legacy memoir: Shortly before her mother died, she had composed a memoir with music and words for her whole family. For years, Rosalie had believed her mother didn't understand or *get* her. But upon hearing her mother's composition, Rosalie realized she was both loved and "seen" with real accuracy by her mother. "My mother's memoir was most healing," Rosalie explained, "and it changed everything for me."

Remember how we said that you're ageless, and so never too old to start your memoir? By the same token, you're never too young. Where is it written that you have to be an elder before beginning? Start right now. Keep a journal and collect whatever feels like important memorabilia. Young people are already blogging and leaving other legacies online—on Facebook, Twitter, Instagram, and multitudinous other social media sites.

If you begin writing your life stories when you're young, imagine how much material you can leave as a legacy for others to learn from and enjoy. An old Chinese proverb says that the best time to plant a tree was forty years ago. The second best time—is today.

PUBLISHING TIPS

You might wonder why we've included anything about publishing in this chapter when, presumably, many writers of legacy memoirs have no intention of publishing them. It's in case you or someone else, upon reading your memoir says: "Dammit, this is good," and you change your mind. Even if your legacy memoir is not published in your lifetime, it may be grist for the memoir of one of your descendants. Your children may well become your biographers or weave your life story into their own. Leave them the gift of who you are.

Exercises: Leaving a Legacy

1) Organize your favorite scrapbook, and group photos together by theme, not time period. For example, "romantic relationships" or "travels" or "places I've lived." Tell a story about each series of photos.

2) Create a legacy box into which you put memorabilia you think you might need for your memoir. Decorate it and cherish it.

3) Write your own obituary as if for publication, as did Jane Catherine Lotter. Give it to someone in the next generation, and when they ask questions, use those as starting places for stories.

4) Imagine that you have just one year left to live. What is the most important story you have to tell?

Writing Prompts

When I was young, I couldn't have known that by the time I was _____, I would be _____.

All my life I believed that _____. But it took a _____ for me to realize that _____.

I come from a long line of ancestors who were _____. I've broken with that pattern by _____.

PART 2

GETTING SERIOUS ABOUT PUBLISHING

It's great to write for yourself, but if you want to publish, you have to reach further.

~**DONNA SEAMAN,** *BOOKLIST* **CRITIC**

Writing a book and publishing a book are two different things. The first involves craft; and the second involves craft plus the knowledge that helps you navigate either traditional or indie publishing. Writers are often notorious for their lack of knowledge about the publishing industry. So here, in this chapter, we'll prepare you for launching your book into the wider world.

Part 2 includes a model cover letter to an editor, "The Perfect Pitch," "Your Literary Friend," on finding an agent, and "Your Book Proposal," with a sample. A book proposal is a vital selling tool for an author looking for a publisher. Also, Brenda includes here several published essays on indie publishing, since she is now a "hybrid author," who publishes both traditionally and with her own publishing house, Delphinius Publishing.

Even if you have a publisher, you still will navigate much of your own publicity to assure that your book doesn't disappear after the initial three months of marketing support that most publishers give new books. If through your marketing efforts and those of the publisher your book takes off, the publisher will be a creative and enthusiastic partner. As Sarah Jane tells her clients, a publisher won't necessarily create a best seller—but they will definitely support one. If you are submitting to publishers or considering indie publishing, there are just as many pitfalls as rewards. We'd like to spare you some of the missteps in this business, which is still a gentleman's (and gentlewoman's) endeavor, but also a rapidly changing and often inscrutable industry.

Unless you attend expensive writing conferences, authors rarely meet the editors, agents, and reviewers who often determine their careers and livelihood. So we asked several of the best editors, book reviewers, and publishers in the business to offer their insights. And we include them here in Part 2.

When your life story moves from friends and family out into the world, one of the first things to consider is your audience. As any listener to NPR will attest, the appetite for personal story telling is enormous. From Ira Glass's *This American Life* to the enduring *Prairie Home Companion* series to the edgy *Snap Judgment*, huge audiences are tuning in to hear people tell the stories of their lives. The same is true for publishing memoir.

No one knows exactly why novels in this new century are fast being replaced by memoir. Perhaps it's because we are more isolated by technology, or because blogging is the primary point of view on the Internet and we are simply in the age of personal realism. Maybe we are weary of celebrity memoirs with their lack of wisdom and elite lives and much more curious about the everyday woes and triumphs of a recognizable life. In an age of social networking, people are practically living online, so we have expanded our kinship systems.

15.
BETTER BLOGGING

Much of blogging is memoir. And everybody's doing it. What used to be a rather private "Dear diary" in a favorite Moleskine notebook is now living out loud—online! Blogging is fun, informative, and sometimes even addictive. But a blog is not a book. It's immediate, in-the-moment "what's up" and often here today, gone tomorrow. Because of its immediacy, blogging often lacks the structure, depth, and narrative arc of a fine memoir. Yet blogging is an entertaining medium in an increasingly wired world.

Popular bloggers often try out new ideas or even stories online and enjoy the responses of an interactive audience. Those who blog or tweet about their lives sometimes attract so many followers, that there's a ready-made audience for a memoir. In fact, blogging can actually be training for your book. Blog posts are a short, self-contained canvas. Working with these manageable bits, you can practice finding your voice, mining your major themes, even discovering your life's epiphanies. If you read any good blog over time, you'll see the writer growing and changing, just like the memoirist.

"Blog away," we always advise our writers. But remember that your blog will have to metamorphose into a memoir with a narrative arc, deepening plot, and characters, and a voice that will engage readers for longer than a coffee break. And if you are blogging your life story, be sure to keep something back for the book. Brenda's mentor, Rachel MacKenzie, warned her to be "wary of a ruinous correspondence," because she'd seen many fine writers give away too much in letters, instead of on the "real page of the book." Rachel's already arched eyebrows might have become permanently raised if she were alive to see today's mania for blogging.

A few bloggers manage to actually turn their blogs into a book, but that is the exception rather than the rule. Mostly we tell our writers, "Blogging is not writing." When best-selling author Diane Johnson met Brenda at a French restaurant in San Francisco when she was on her book tour for *Le Divorce*, she was the first to explain the phenomenon of blogging to Brenda: "You just get online," Diane said with a sigh, "and go blah, blah, blah." And she was right. So much of blogging is *blah, blah, blahing*. Even though we may post to Facebook or tweet our favorite blog links, how many published blog collections have you actually read?

Maybe you are blogging for fun, or for other bloggers, because you have an interest in a particular subject or cause. If, however, you're blogging or keeping a website with the possibility of getting published, then you have to think about what you're doing in a more writerly way. It is no longer just for you, for friends and like-minded folk. Your blog has to have a more professional, polished, and universal appeal.

When Robert Rummel-Hudson, author of the poignant, funny, and beautifully written memoir *Schuyler's Monster: A Father's Journey with His Wordless Daughter*, first got in touch with Sarah Jane, he had a successful website. It was obvious from the beginning that Robert could write, but his manuscript read like his blog: episodic, disjointed, self-deprecating, and relentlessly funny in a sitcom sort of way. What it lacked were many of the important elements necessary for a book: backstory, continuity, intimacy—and real, vivid narrative.

Sarah Jane suggested that Robert start afresh—forget the blog and begin to tell the story of his experiences with a remarkable child who taught him about living and loving and overcoming. What a difference! After rewriting and revising, Sarah Jane read a finished manuscript about a man who became *every* parent, and a child who became *our* child. St. Martin's Press published the book, which came out first in hardcover and then in paperback.

Blogging is like journalism—yes, it is a kind of egalitarian journalism. It can often train your writing style into the same rise-and-fall format of a newspaper columnist. For years, Brenda has worked with what she calls "recovering journalists." From a *Los Angeles Times* reporter, Leslie Helm, who after several years published a memoir, *Yokohama Yankee: My Family's Five Generations as Outsiders in Japan*, to a former *BusinessWeek* reporter, Dori Jones Yang, who has a second successful career publishing novels and nonfiction, both with traditional and indie publishers. Like many journalists whose first-person point of view has long been censored in favor of "just the facts," many reporters have to coax a personal narrator on to the page again and again; memoir is not reporting on others' points of view. Even though many bloggers are writing in first person, there is often a reportorial slant in their writings, much like "opinion page" prose. If you are a passionate blogger, you must look beyond your persuasive skills or daily preoccupations to discover your personal story in book-length form. Or else you'll be a "recovering blogger."

Good storytelling has not changed because neither has the human heart.

WHY A BLOG IS NOT YET A BOOK

In a blog, your thoughts, stories, and epiphanies are instantly broadcast. There is little editing or rewriting or craft. Readers comment or criticize just as quickly. While this is all very exhilarating, it can also distract, limit, and interrupt the serious memoirist. As a character in the 2011 movie *Contagion* quips: "Blogging is not writing. It's just graffiti with punctuation."

Just because you have a blog with many "hits" doesn't mean you have the material you need for a good memoir. Blogs are great to jump-start a writer, to float ideas, gather an audience, and dash off daily stories or insights. But you'll find that if you collect all of your blog posts together, they do not equal a book or a memoir. They are pieces, not a whole. For that, time and real reflection is required. Memoir is a craft, not a momentary realization. It builds chapter by chapter with an organizing intelligence always aware of the big picture. Blogging is like an instant story, and often it lasts no longer than that.

In a popular *Atlantic* cover story, "Is Google Making Us Stupid?," author Nicholas Carr notes that Internet blogs are "a different kind of reading, and behind it lies a different kind of thinking—perhaps even a new sense of the self." Often blogs are just a bare-bones sense of the self—like a Cliff's Notes version of your life.

Even though Brenda has a blog and writes regularly for the *Huffington Post*, she advises her students when they have an idea: *Write first, blog later*. The impulse for a blog post and the attention span of its readers is much less substantial than a chapter. Reading a blog is more like surfing than settling into an ocean cruise. Even successful bloggers, when they sit down to try and write a book, often fail.

BLOGS THAT BECOME BOOKS

There are, however, some very popular bloggers who successfully transformed their personal blogs into a book. Some of the most frequented blogs are those whose eccentric, darkly comic voices are addictive. You return to them just as you would a daily or weekly columnist in your favorite newspaper. Jenny Lawson, "The Bloggess," turned her snarky and entertaining blog, illustrated by family snapshots, into the best-selling memoir *Let's Pretend This Never Happened*. Lawson's blog was selected by *Time* magazine in 2013 as number one on their list of "The 25 Best Bloggers." They described Lawson's voice like this: "Think David Sedaris in hot rollers or Neil Gaiman if he liked to swear and had grown up in Texas with a father who was a professional taxidermist."

Her memoir reads like a series of blogs, but it does have a narrative arc—from a screamingly funny childhood through a charmingly comic fifteen-year marriage anchored by the witty angst of motherhood. If you are hoping for humor in your own life story, take a look at Lawson, along with David Sedaris, whose NPR vignettes, like an audio blog, launched his wildly successful career in memoir.

Also take a look at the blogger Allie Brosh, whose book, *Hyperbole and a Half: Unfortunate Situations, Flawed Coping Mechanisms, Mayhem, and Other Things That Happened*, is drawn from her blog. Brosh's idiosyncratic drawings and ruminations attract five million visitors a month. Like Lawson, Brosh struggles with chronic depression and anxiety, but in a narrative voice that is at once absurd and engaging. Brosh is a monologist or chatty cartoonist more than a memoirist. Her chapters are illustrated scenes, brief and episodic, but often very moving. When a woman gives her a weird look at a video store, Brosh assumes it is "because I looked really depressed and I was dressed like an Eskimo vagrant.

Normally, I would have felt an instant, crushing sense of self-consciousness, but instead, I felt nothing."

TIPS FOR BETTER BLOGGING

If you're wondering whether, like Brosh and Lawson, your blog can be turned into a book, study some of the blogs you most admire and then see if they've been compiled and published as a memoir. Look at how the narrator's voice changes, or not, from blog to book. Read over several years of a blog to see if there is the essential evolution of character that makes a successful memoir. Observe how you're reading the blog. Do you sit down and read entry after entry, as if they were chapters, or is it episodic scanning like many online sites? Do you settle in to the blog as if it were book-length? Does it have a compelling plot? Or is it repetition of the same conflict? Most of all, do you keep on reading because you want to be closer to the main character? Are you learning anything about life?

To discover how to convert your blog into a book, print out fifty pages of your best blogs. Read them together as if they are a whole, not just parts. See if there is an organizing principle, either chronological or thematic. Can you see a way to organize them as a memoir, not just episodes in your life? Is there a beginning, middle, and end to the drama? Do the blogs make real chapters that flow, or do you need to add connective tissue between them to make sense? Do you, as a memoirist, grow and change over time?

Remember, even if you have a zillion subscribers to your blog, there will be new readers for your book who have no history or connection to your story. So you have to do what all memoirists must do, tell them a well-crafted story from beginning to end. Hold their attention, not just with episodic wit or "slices of life," but also with a well-shaped storyline.

DIGITAL NATION

For those of you who do much of your reading online, we recommend the free *Publishing Perspectives* for daily news about all forms of publishing. Mediabistro also gives a wonderful, eclectic, and trusted glimpse into publishing. A recent *New York Times Book Review* article, "Writing Bytes," was a roundup of what several well-known authors think about how modern technology might change the nature of storytelling. Even though each of these authors writes in a very different style—from futuristic to historical fiction, thrillers, humor, poetry, essays, and even science fiction—and even though their ages vary from thirty-five to midseventies, as novelist Dana Spiotta says, "Technology changes everything—and nothing."

That seems to be the general consensus for those of us who've spent our careers in publishing. Good storytelling has not changed, because neither has the human heart, which ultimately is what all storytelling is about. What has changed is that what you write has to read as if it is current and up-to-date. (See Chapter Notes, page 253, for web links to *Publishing Perspectives*, Mediabistro, *GalleyCat*, and the articles on the best bloggers and the technology of writing.)

What has also changed is that today, more than ever, writers must be organized and disciplined in their quest to discover inventive ways to unplug and enter that world of deep reflection and solitude—that inner world where you get in touch with your own basic humanity, and your characters'. Regardless of technology, inner life is ultimately the power that drives us. This confirms what Sarah Jane always tells clients who are concerned about the future of publishing: "The medium you use to read (or listen to) might change, but the basic human need for story and story tellers never will. If you tell a good story and write well, you will always have an audience. Remember, there must once have been a time when a writer said: 'It's *not* coming out as an illuminated manuscript? What do you mean it's only going to be *printed*? Who will read that?'"

So if you're already blogging your life story, don't give yourself away. Think of blogging as singing scales in preparation for the real concert to come. Think of it as your "life story lite," with the best scenes saved for your memoir. If you practice a little bit of narrative abstinence and hold back the best for your book, then you can use your blog to support your book rather than letting your blog dissipate it. Readers may respond to your free blog with pleasure, comments, and demand for more. But you want them to return and commit to buy your book. Blogs are one-night stands or at the best, romantic affairs. Books are committed relationships.

16.
AGENTS

THE PERFECT PITCH: WRITING A QUERY LETTER

(Adapted from Sarah Jane's website)

I'm a literary agent who, truth be told, doesn't actually believe in "the pitch." My gut reaction to the question "What is the perfect pitch?" is to answer, Zen-like, "The perfect pitch . . . is no pitch."

Which is why I decided to look up the verb *pitch* in the dictionary—and this is what I found: "to put, set, or plant in a fixed or definite position; to deliver to serve to the batter; to determine the key or keynote of a melody; to attempt to sell or win approval for, promote, advertise, i.e. to pitch breakfast foods at a sales conference—politicians pitching on TV." Maybe it's the breakfast-cereal-and-politicians-on-TV aspect of pitching that turns me off, although the concept of hitting the perfect note of a melody is intriguing.

While I am not interested in your selling me anything, I *am* willing to be seduced, amazed, charmed, or moved. What I really want is for you to share your enthusiasm with me, your passion—to invite me along on a journey; to tell me something you, and you alone, know; to open my eyes to a truth that will enable me to see the world in a different way. And, of course, to do so with beautiful writing.

> *Invite me along on a journey. Tell me something you alone know.*

As the e-mails arrive every day, I am not so naive, so high-minded, or so much of a romantic to ignore the fact that only a few clearly grab my attention, while most others fall either flat or overinflated on the screen.

So what is it about the approach that works? What are the elements of the successful pitch? To begin with, let's face it: we're talking about writing. The importance of elegant, finely honed writing—even in the introductory e-mail—cannot be overstated. Nor, for that matter, can all the other aspects of good professional writing, such as spelling, punctuation, grammar, and so on.

And while there are no hard-and-fast rules, I've formed the following preferences over the years:

Write; don't call. If you are introducing yourself and "pitching" an unsolicited work, do so with a query letter via e-mail. This gives you the opportunity to organize your thoughts, list your credentials, and provide a flavor of your writing style. It also gives me the opportunity to digest, ponder, and reread what you've written. If, however, you insist on calling, introduce yourself and tell me what you do and how it relates to your book; and be prepared with a good story and a clear, succinct description of your idea.

I represent quite a few spiritual book authors, and so I get calls from people who (more often than I can believe) say: "Hello. I've written the most amazing book about my spiritual experience." And when I venture to ask what it's about, the answer I get is usually a variation on the following: "Umm, well, it's a new look at God, and human beings, and our relationship to the universe."

There is someone, on the other hand, who calls me every few months—a lovely woman from somewhere down south—and she is forgiven. Because with a voice that sounds like Dolly Parton, she refers to me as "Miz Sarah," and while I have never formally taken her on as a client, I have read the revisions of her manuscript for going on three years now. And she never fails to tell me how she is praying for me and for the entire city of New York. And I do believe she is.

Also, it doesn't hurt to do a little research on the categories each agent prefers. You'll save yourself a lot of time by targeting the right agents for your work. You can do this by looking in *Publishers Marketplace* or in *Jeff Herman's Guide to Book Publishers, Editors, and Literary Agents*. And please, don't under any circumstance be tempted to resort to gimmicks—ostrich feathers, scented candles, cutesy stationary, aromatherapy (or snake) oil, wands, cat pawprints, dried flowers, or family photographs—all of which, and more, I have received. What those little enticements say to me is that you don't have faith in your own material.

Be outrageous if you will, but be dignified about it. Once we have begun working together and I have sold your book, then you can send me chocolates, flowers, potpourri, artisanal cheeses, or other thoughtful gifts. One of my charming authors has sent me an orchid for each of her books I've sold. Another used to bring me freshly laid eggs from her hens whenever she came to New York (back when one was still allowed to fly with eggs).

I am drawn to authors who, in their introductory letters, demonstrate that they are confident but not boastful. It's not a good idea to praise your own work and tell me how wonderful your book is. It is, however, helpful to list your credentials and make the connection for me between what you do, what you know, and what you chose to write about. And that's as true for fiction as it is for non-fiction. It always amazes me how the flavor comes across in a query—not only of the work, but also of many of the personality traits of the author. Whenever prospective clients start their e-mail with "I am looking for a New York literary agent who will aggressively market my book," I read no further. I have learned from experience that this is not the kind of client I am interested in working with.

Being a literary agent is not just my work. For me, the line between work, books, writers, ideas, and my life, is blurred. Many of the authors I represent have become personal friends—friends with whom my family and I have had the good fortune to share something of the world about which they write. One such sharing was the journey my husband and I took with my author to experience firsthand the magic of the "friendly" Pacific gray whales off the coast of Baja California; they actually come up to your boat to make contact with humans and to be touched. I have also spent time meditating with one of my authors in a Zen Buddhist monastery. I have stayed with one of my cookbook authors on the rugged Greek island where she and her husband now live and where she is writing her next book. I have traveled and given a writing workshop with another of my clients while she gave a photography workshop in Mexico. And with one of my more intrepid authors, I climbed New Hampshire's Mount Monadnock on the hottest day of that year.

Wonderful one-liners are rare and hard to come by. But if you're able to sum up your entire book with either a terrific title or an attention-grabbing one-line description—that's gold. So before you send off that final draft of your pitch e-mail, let your intuitive imagination run wild. Get together with clever friends and see if you can come up with a delicious one-liner that says it all.

In addition to terrific writing, there is another quality I really value and always look for—a quality that often shines through, even in an e-mail: authenticity. By authenticity, I mean the assurance and dignity that comes from being genuinely knowledgeable and truly intimate with the subject you are writing about. It's clear that you've immersed yourself in it, that you've walked the walk so you can talk the talk (or write the write). This authenticity makes me feel as if a book *had* to be written. Not just because the author would love to be published, but also because the author has something important to say, something to add to the world. And from a practical point of view, this authenticity helps with another key aspect of a good pitch—clear focus and good organization.

And what about honesty? If, for instance, along with your pitch letter you enclose all the kind, beautifully written rejection letters you have received from other agents, you've told me too much. I am surprised at how often would-be authors do that. Maybe they feel the rejections are an indication of how close they've come to being accepted. But the only thing it says to me is how thoughtful most agents are. On the other hand, if you don't tell me that, under another title your book was sent out by another agent and rejected by twenty publishers, then you haven't told me enough.

I would love to share with you some of the effective pitch letters I have received, but there is no cookie-cutter approach to writing a good query. Provided you write well and are coming from an authentic place, everything else is up for grabs. You can be as provocative, outrageous, sentimental, cynical, vulnerable, or humorous as you choose—whatever reflects who you are and what you have to say.

Also, I say with absolute conviction that, as with everything else in life, so much of what transpires between an author, an agent, and a book is timing and chemistry. Your eyes meet someone else's—on the street as you're waiting for a bus, on the beach, in an art gallery, across the proverbial crowded room, on a ledge hanging off a mountain cliff—and something clicks. In other words, one either falls in love, or doesn't. This, in my opinion, holds as true for books as it does for people.

And when that "click" happens and a spark is ignited, one tends to rationalize: it was that charming query, the subject is so timely, the author has such a fabulous voice, it's such a great title, and so on and so forth. But for me the truth, alas and thank goodness, is both simpler and more mysterious. And what can any of us do about chemistry? It's something over which neither you nor I have any control. I often hear clients say, "What will be will be." And while I believe in the mysterious, I refuse to accept that *que sera, sera* approach. When it comes to writing, as one of my clients always says, "Trust in God, but tether your camel." So take responsibility for all the advice listed in this book, and the mysterious will take care of itself.

By the way, if you would like to know more about how to create an "open sesame" query, there are countless books that will tell you how. The best, in Sarah Jane's opinion, is agent Katharine Sands's *Making the Perfect Pitch: How to Catch a Literary Agent's Eye.*

YOUR BOOK PROPOSAL

Here's a typical scenario: a writer sends an agent, such as Sarah Jane, a short but descriptive query letter regarding their memoir (or any nonfiction book for that matter). The author's pitch letter hits all the right notes. Sarah Jane is intrigued and says she'd be happy to take a look. The author is thrilled and confident that the book is on its way. But not so fast. Just as the author is celebrating this next major step, Sarah Jane e-mails and says: "You have a proposal and sample chapters, right?"

"A proposal?" you wonder. "I have the complete manuscript, the finished memoir, so why would I need a proposal? And what is it? What does it do? And how would I put one together?"

What many writers don't realize is that all nonfiction books are sold on the basis of a proposal and sample chapters. Agents and editors won't even look at a prospective nonfiction book unless it's submitted in that form. They're just too busy to read every manuscript they receive, and a proposal includes information that helps an agent make the decision whether or not to read the entire book and take a chance on representing it. For an editor, a proposal provides important information that helps them decide whether or not to buy it.

Creating an effective proposal requires specific skills. For some writers, these come easily, but for others—even for talented and published authors—writing a proposal is a real ordeal. If you try doing it several times and just can't seem to get it right, Sarah Jane advises paying a professional independent editor to write it for you.

Think of a proposal as the blueprint for your book, or as the skeleton upon which you build muscle, sinew, and tissue. Also think of it as a sales document, pointing out the information that can set you apart—not with tired words like *thrilling, insightful, groundbreaking, moving,* and on and on—but with the facts, details, specifics, and information that can differentiate you.

Here are the elements that go into a proposal:

1) **OVERVIEW**—a summary of the whole book, very much like the query letter you sent the agent.

2) **ABOUT THE AUTHOR**—in which you mention your current (or previous) job, your platform, any previous books you've written and published, and, if relevant, your marketing skills and connections.

3) **THE COMPETITION**—where you discuss what's out there that's similar and why yours is better. It's fine, by the way (if you can substantiate it) to explain why there's nothing quite like what you've written.

4) TABLE OF CONTENTS (OR TOC)—each chapter with a descriptive paragraph. Often, when actually writing the book, chapters can change and shift a bit. That's okay.

5) WORD COUNT AND ESTIMATED DELIVERY DATE—how long (approximately) you think your book will be, and when you believe you'll be able to deliver it. Many authors have actually written the entire manuscript before even putting the proposal together. But this is not always necessary.

6) INTRODUCTION AND SAMPLE CHAPTERS—Sarah Jane generally advises that you send two or three consecutive chapters so an editor or agent can get a sense of continuity. At this stage, it's fine to use copyrighted materials, which might, in your finished book, need permissions.

Not counting the sample chapters, which are often an additional fifty to seventy-five pages, a proposal is generally between twenty-five and thirty-five pages long. After reading the proposal and sample chapters, if Sarah Jane (or any other agent) believes this is a book she feels good about, she and the author sign an author-agent agreement, which covers the rights and responsibilities of each. Then Sarah Jane gives the author editorial feedback. Sarah Jane can't remember the last time she sent out a book without any suggestions to make it better. Like with editors, there are some agents who simply acquire or sign up, and agents, like Sarah Jane, who edit. You are fortunate if you have an agent who takes the time to personally help shape and edit your book.

These days, agents send out proposals electronically, along with the agent's own cover letter that explains what the book is about and entices editor interest. Unless the agent has a specific publisher in mind, the proposal is sent out to many editors at once. It can easily take a month or so for editors to respond, and sometimes, no matter how many nice reminders, the editor never does. Sadly, that nonresponse can be read as a rejection. But keep trying, because the opinions of agents and editors are subjective, and there are many examples of best-selling authors, like J. K. Rowling (scribbling away at a local pub), John Grisham (whose first novel was not a best seller), and Stephen King (whose wife rescued his manuscript from the trash), who received many rejections before finding the right agent and editor for their work.

SARAH JANE'S COVER LETTER TO EDITOR

Here is the cover letter that Sarah Jane sent to editors with Brenda's book proposal for *I Want to Be Left Behind*. Merloyd Lawrence, at Da Capo Press/Perseus Books Group, bought it.

Dear Merloyd,

Brenda Peterson's *I Want to Be Left Behind: Finding Rapture Here on Earth* is a memoir of life lived at the intersection of two modern American cultures: Christians preparing for The Rapture, and environmentalists and climate change scientists who are trying to save the planet before it's too late.

But this isn't a memoir of religious guilt or global warming panic—it's an often wry, sometimes hilarious, unusually tender look at life within these two modern milieus. "There are no drowning polar bears or melting ice caps where I'm going," a relative assures her, but Brenda is unconvinced. And the ubiquitous "In case of Rapture, this car will be unmanned" bumper sticker is met with Brenda's own: "In case of Rapture, can I have your car?"

Maybe it's her mother's "revelatory" ice cream; maybe it's her father's influence: his forestry teachings and his deep devotion to their animals. Or maybe it's just Brenda's intuitive belief that the animals that mean so much to her cannot be soulless, disposable beings. But, whatever the reason, Brenda simply cannot follow her family's Southern Baptist religion, which teaches that this world is worth abandoning—and, thus, begins her journey.

From Bible memorization drills to environmental activism, childhood revivals to 1970s Berkeley radicals, Brenda's journey is one exploring the two polarized viewpoints of modern America—evolving, ultimately, into a compassionate look at two dominant forces in American life today.

Brenda's previous work, the darkly comic novel *Duck and Cover* (Harper Collins, 1991), was a *New York Times* Notable Book of the Year. Her *Build Me an Ark: A Life with Animals* (Norton, 2001) was selected as Best Spiritual Book by *Spirituality & Health* magazine.

Her work has appeared in the *New York Times, Chicago Tribune, San Francisco Chronicle, Reader's Digest, Christian Science Monitor,* and *Utne Reader.* Brenda's website is: http://www.brendapetersonbooks.com.

Here is the first chapter of the book, published in *Orion* magazine: www.orionmagazine.org/index.php/articles/article/502. I look forward to hearing from you.

Sincerely,
Sarah Jane
Sarah Jane Freymann Literary Agency

We sold *I Want to Be Left Behind* in March 2009 and delivered the manuscript to the publisher in December that same year. It was published in February 2010. This was a very tight turnaround, even for Brenda; she had to write flat out to make her deadline.

Sarah Jane always recommends, especially for first-time authors, that they ask for as much time from the publisher as possible, as much as two years, if the agent can negotiate this. You will need all the time you can get for revision, editing, and then preparing for publication. Good luck with your own proposal!

YOUR LITERARY FRIEND

Everyone needs an editor. Everyone. No matter what you are writing or how long you have been doing it—you need an editor. Why? Because you wrote what you saw in your mind, and what you saw there was absolutely perfect. Perfect because you thought about it, planned it, constructed it, and worked it. And you're right; it is absolutely perfect. Perfect with one enormous "if"—if you are the only person who is ever going to read it. But if you intend to show it to anyone else, your obligation moves from solely saying what *you* want to say and how *you* want to say it to considering what other people want to read and how they want to read it. Obviously, this is most true if you want to be published.

Pick up any one of the five last books you read (or the last fifteen or the last twenty-five) and go to the acknowledgments section. Various names will be mentioned for various reasons, but what every one of those books has in common is a thank-you to two people—the writer's agent and the writer's editor.

Seasoned published writers know this isn't simply good PR or recognition because it's expected; those thank-yous are there because without the agent's and editor's contributions, the book would never have been published: a thank-you to the agent for helping to shape the manuscript (or proposal) before even trying to sell it, and one to the editor for putting the manuscript into its final form.

And these days one can make a case that the agent is the more important of the two. Since editors are increasingly busy and frequently move around from publisher to publisher, the agent is often a writer's most trusted and loyal literary friend.

This reminds Sarah Jane of a story she heard a spiritual teacher tell:

A man traveling across the barren desert suddenly sees a brilliant green oasis on the horizon. *Is it real or an apparition?* As he gets closer, he sees that he is in the midst of a verdant, lush garden. Birds sing in the trees, bees hum, and colorful butterflies collect nectar. There are flowers blooming; vegetables, corn and wheat growing; and luscious fruit hanging heavily on the vine. The man sees a cottage nestled in the shade and knocks on the door. A woman emerges, and the aroma of freshly baked bread wafts his way. Dazzled, the wanderer says, "How blessed you are that God has shined all these gifts upon you." The woman smiles and says, "You are right, of course. But you should have seen this place when God had it all to himself."

And so it is with a book—before the agent and editor get to shape, glaze, and bake the literary dough.

It is as amazing to Sarah Jane (as it is to her authors) the difference between what writers often believe the subject of their book is, and what Sarah Jane knows it to be. As her mind works in a somewhat linear fashion, when she comes upon holes and unanswered questions in the story, her curiosity is aroused. She needs those holes filled and those questions answered. Often, it's only after seeing what's missing that Sarah Jane says she "gets" it—that she understands what the story *really* is (or should be) about. As Mark Twain commented: "The time to begin an article is when you have finished it to your satisfaction. By that time you begin to clearly and logically perceive what it is you really want to say."

Sometimes, "getting it" is ineffable and intangible. Even Sarah Jane can be surprised by the discovery. Not unlike her father who was a doctor and a great diagnostician, she suddenly knows what is wrong with the manuscript and how to make it right. Interestingly, she often finds herself homing in on the problem while engaged in doing something completely different, like walking in the park, or working out at the gym, or just spacing out.

This, however, is an experience you can't fake or hurry along; it comes with time and dedication to the process. To illustrate this process, Sarah Jane (the agent) and Margaret Combs (the author, who generously agreed to participate in writing this chapter) tell the story of working on Margaret's memoir-in-progress, *Hazard: A Memoir of Family, Flight, and Forgiveness*, from their individual perspectives.

HOW AN AGENT AND AUTHOR WORK TOGETHER

This is a real example of how an agent and writer work together to create a proposal for editors. It's from the point of view of the agent and then the author.

Agent Sarah Jane Freymann's Point of View

It started with a memoir workshop in Seattle during which Brenda introduced me to her students. Among them was Margaret, an award-winning NPR journalist. Margaret was working on a memoir about growing up as the "other child." Because her brother, Roddy, was born with autism, he became the focus of the family. She carried these feelings of being an outsider with her into adulthood. Impressive as her platform was, I would have been far more intrigued had this been a memoir by the parent of an autistic child, or about a new treatment for autism, or a story about the love between an autistic brother and his healthy sister.

Then I read the sample chapters. Wow, they were gorgeous. Margaret wrote beautifully and evocatively. She made an entire world come alive: I saw her pretty and intense mother, her handsome, reserved, but caring father. I met Margaret's old-fashioned, loving grandparents. I saw a delighted family bringing home their adorable firstborn son and the scene, in which Margaret's mother collapses, when she learns that something is terribly wrong with her little boy.

From these chapters, I got a whole new perspective and a surprise: Margaret was not the only sister. She had a slightly older sibling, Becky Ann. This older sister had done many of the same things Margaret had, and had done them even *before* her. I told Margaret how surprised I was to discover that she'd had a fun and loving relationship with an older sister and suggested that the memoir make that clear early on. I also didn't quite see, at first, how the autistic younger brother was such a catalyst. In my opinion, her memoir told the story of the quintessential middle-American family.

Margaret reworked the manuscript and sent it back to me. This time the sister, who was spunky and clearly a buddy, made much more of an appearance. But I wondered, quietly—because I didn't even want to admit it to myself—what's the story here? Also, reading the chapters, there was something new bothering me: too much "beautiful writing." It might seem odd to readers, but the writing, although lovely, was impeding the narrative flow. There were simply too many descriptions and too much interior. I wanted to get on with the story; and this version was like taking two steps forward and two (granted, very well-written) steps back.

So I did exactly what I often advise authors to do. I turned to something else. I went into the kitchen, made myself a cup of tea, and stirred the fresh tomato sauce I was making from a recipe my friend, Luigi, had given me. I honestly wasn't aware of thinking about anything other than basil, garlic, and chili flakes when out of the blue I knew what the story was *really* about, and why Margaret's memoir was important.

Margaret had been telling this story of autism from the perspective of our contemporary consciousness and from life in the open-minded, enlightened city of Seattle. I had been reading and evaluating it through a similar lens—Manhattan in 2013.

But this story took place sixty years ago. At first, when her mother realized that something was wrong, there wasn't even a diagnosis of autism. The boy was considered "retarded." In that time, unlike today, there were no support groups, no community of parents with similar issues, no special schools, no books, and no specific diets and—especially—no hope. Margaret's younger brother was not one of those interesting, quirky, yet highly functioning autistic people such as Temple Grandin or Naoki Higashida, author of *The Reason I Jump: The Inner Voice of a Thirteen-Year-Old Boy with Autism*. Margaret's brother was more severely impaired and this affected every member of the family.

In the 1950s and '60s in Kentucky and Colorado, this was a family who would have been completely isolated in their loss and their grief. No wonder those two spunky, healthy sisters wanted nothing more than to escape home as quickly as possible. To go out with boys, go to movies, do all the things that were forbidden in their strict, strongly religious, borderline fundamentalist home. From the moment they realized something was wrong with Roddy, every member of the family was overburdened with this grief. So even though it was Margaret writing this memoir, the story wasn't just about her—it was about an entire family's disorienting pain. Now, I understood its relevance.

I was so excited about sharing my insights with Margaret that although it was almost 10:00 p.m. in New York City and she was on a ferry crossing Puget Sound, I left several messages on her cell phone.

It's not always easy—scratch that—it's *never* easy to hear your work being judged. What I've noticed, however, is that the more seasoned the writer, the more open they are to hearing what I, or another agent or editor, has to say. So it was with Margaret. She's a real pro, and she listened and was appreciative. It was a gratifying experience for me. I hope it was for her as well. (See Chapter Notes, page 253, for a link to Margaret's website.)

Author Margaret Combs's Point of View

When I first started writing my book about growing up with my autistic brother, I didn't know where to begin. I just knew a book didn't exist like the one I wanted to write. Though I had come from a reportorial career as a producer and host for NPR, I had never worked on a book-length manuscript. And I had no sense of a beginning or an end—partly because neither existed for me. I didn't fully remember my brother's birth—I was too young—and I don't yet know the end, since he is still living and his reverberations continue even now.

It wasn't until I happened to join a memoir workshop at my local library, with Brenda Peterson, that I found the beginning. She gave an assignment to write one scene that explained my whole life. I wrote about the day I saw my mother collapse after learning that my brother was "brain-damaged." Shortly after I joined Brenda's ongoing class I brought in a series of memories—each two to ten lines or so—punching home the most vivid and dramatic moments that lingered from my childhood.

Thanks to Brenda, I learned how to flesh out these memories into scenes and into chapters, and soon I was able to get a few stories published in literary magazines like *North American Review.* When I had several chapters written and an annotated table of contents, Brenda suggested we begin to test the waters for an agent. This is where my learning curve shot upward. From all of the books I had absorbed about submitting to an agent, I thought I knew the process of how it worked and what to expect. I had the impression that you submitted your chapters, credentials, best sales pitch, and then waited an inordinate amount of time and, if you were fortunate, got a reply, yes or no. The agent, in my mind, was someone who said, "I'll look over your proposal and, if I can sell it, as is, I'll send you a contract."

In my experience, this couldn't have been further from the truth. Sarah Jane Freymann responded to me several times. She did not commit to taking my book proposal, but talked about what would strengthen it. In other words, she worked more like an editor. The first time, she wanted to understand more about the character of me as a child—to connect more with me emotionally and to see my movement forward from chapter to chapter. The second time, she wanted me to rewrite my author's note or pitch letter. She felt I had written a pitch for another book, a how-to book on autism. My book was about a family—"a quintessential American story"—and she wanted to get this from the pitch letter and the annotated table of contents. She wanted me to take all of the marketing language out of my pitch letter and write it from the heart. After talking with her, I got back to work.

The third time Sarah Jane spoke to me over the phone, she delivered the words I wanted to hear. "You did it," she said. "I have now found what this book is about." I heard her say my story back to me: *This is the story of a family being out of place at a certain time when autism wasn't known. It's about a time and a place, and a child growing up in a family sixty years ago.* I'd had this concept inside my mind for so long that it moved me to hear it coming back to me in someone else's voice.

Each time Sarah Jane counseled me and I rewrote according to her feedback, I saw the book and the proposal strengthen. With her, I have been in good hands—several pairs of good hands actually—those of an agent, an editor, a coach, and a teacher. I'll never again think of an agent as just an agent.

17.
EDITORS

Grateful credit and praise given to editors in the acknowledgments of any book is well earned. Not only can good editors keep you from looking like a fool in public, they can actually elevate your prose to "its best light." Brenda often says that her books had a happy childhood with her editors. And Sarah Jane's longtime warm, personal relationship with editors has ensured her success as a literary agent.

Since we've worked with some of the most astute editors in publishing, we want to share with you some of their wise advice. Even if you are self-publishing, you will be hiring editors as an invaluable stage of producing a book. Reading the advice of these editors, book critics, and other memoirists is like attending a writers' conference and meeting remarkable publishing pros—but all here on the page.

MARLENE BLESSING

Marlene Blessing is both an author and editor. She has published memoir and edited the classic women's travel book *A Road of Her Own: Women's Journeys in the West*. As editor in chief of Alaska Northwest Books and Fulcrum Publishing, Blessing worked with many memoirists, including Teri Hein, author of *Atomic Farm Girl: Growing Up Right in the Wrong Place*, and Brenda's essay collection, *Living by Water: True Stories of Nature and Spirit*.

Marlene Blessing's Tips for Editing and Improving Your Own Writing

You've written your heart out, and it's all on the page. Now it's time to cut, shape, and polish that gem. First, you'll need to have a great set of tools to help you do the work.

My Favorite Editing Tools

I use these guides again and again:

- *Merriam-Webster's Collegiate Dictionary*, 11th ed., for spelling
- *Eats, Shoots & Leaves* by Lynne Truss, for punctuation (she'll make you laugh as you learn)
- The quirky illustrated version of *The Elements of Style* by Strunk and White, and artist Maira Kalman—for usage and style, and even more fun
- The tasty *The Deluxe Transitive Vampire: The Ultimate Handbook of Grammar for the Innocent, the Eager, and the Doomed* by Karen Elizabeth Gordon (because you never thought you'd find vampires in a grammar guide)

It's also valuable to have a thesaurus (for diction), *Bartlett's Familiar Quotations*, 18th ed. (for eloquent quotes), and an atlas. Plus, online searches, today's speediest research tools—just be sure you're getting your information from a reliable source.

Now, my ten top tips for editing your own writing:

1) **CUT THE FRILLS**: Don't let your own fancy "wordifying" get in the way of a good story. Highlight every uberliterary word, phrase, and sentence in your document. Examine each, one at a time—honesty required!—and delete or revise any that seem there more to trot out your own erudition than to

> *A good editor can keep you from*
> *looking like a fool in public.*

connect your reader to the story. As Stephen King wrote in *On Writing: A Memoir of the Craft*, "Kill your darlings, kill your darlings, even when it breaks your egocentric little scribbler's heart, kill your darlings."

2) DO A "SENSORY AUDIT": For every descriptive passage, check to see if you've given the reader something to see, smell, taste, touch, or hear. Engage at least two senses each time to ensure that you're transporting your reader to a place and time in the most concrete way you can.

3) ORDER, PLEASE!: Create an orderly progression for your reader, even if you plan to zigzag in time in your story. You want your reader to stay on your yellow brick road. Do as many "Save As" versions of your digital document as you need to try out different possibilities. Reword if necessary to improve your new transitions.

4) BEGIN WELL: What if Dickens had opened *A Tale of Two Cities* with "In that period of time, it was considered to be the best and worst of times . . . ," instead of "It was the best of times, it was the worst of times." Be direct whenever possible and grab the reader by the collar with your first sentence.

5) WEED OUT REDUNDANCIES: We all have favorite words and verbal tics. Do a "search" in your document to discover how many times you used, say, the word "opportunity" in an essay on social equality. This is when your thesaurus and dictionary are your best friends. Find as many strong substitutions as you can, and replace your repeats with them.

6) BE ACTIVE: You don't need to nuke every passive verb construction in your writing. Just make sure that you choose active constructions as often as possible to avoid stiffness, formality, and wordiness: "Our group decided . . . ," not "It was decided by our group . . ."

7) ON WHOSE AUTHORITY?: Get your facts straight. Knowledge adds power to your story, whether you're writing fiction, nonfiction, or poetry. A famous poet once advised me: "You must *know* that a bird's bones are hollow." I fact-checked his bit of wisdom and learned that (a) not all bird bones are hollow; (b) the birds with the greatest number of hollow bones are those that soar on thermals; and (c) flightless birds such as penguins don't have any hollow bones. Now I can write about birds.

8) VOICE CHECK: Would your story improve if your narrator were more casual in tone, or witty, tender, imperious, bitter, philosophical, childlike, or uncertain? Even in essays, where you are the narrator, you'll fine-tune your voice to create the kind of appeal you intend (a call to action, sympathy, provocation, laughter, etc.). Word choice is a key aspect of your voice check. Read your piece out loud to yourself and see if you stumble over a logjam of words and a rushing river of ideas. Then try to clear the path.

9) METAPHORICALLY SPEAKING: A good metaphor gives the reader a hit of verbal java. Too many verbal fireworks might make your reader dizzy, but a few original dazzlers in your writing will lift their spirits.

10) THE FINAL POLISH: Back to your tools! Check spelling, grammar, word usage, punctuation, capitalization, paragraph breaks, and any other nit you can think of. You have the tools.

Now have some fun polishing your writing to a fine shine!

MERLOYD LAWRENCE

Merloyd Lawrence has long been a revered name in publishing. Now she has her own prestigious imprint, Da Capo Press, under the publishing umbrella of Perseus Books. Several of her books have had a profound effect on health and culture—from *The Boy Who Loved Windows: Opening the Heart and Mind of a Child Threatened With Autism* to *Dr. Susan Love's Breast Book* to *Raising Elijah: Protecting Our Children in an Age of Environmental Crisis*. Lawrence has also edited the popular memoirs *When I Was Puerto Rican*, *Song Without Words: Discovering My Deafness Halfway through Life*, and *Pigs Can't Swim*, as well as Brenda's memoir *I Want to Be Left Behind*. (See Chapter Notes, page 253, for a web link to for more of her books.) Brenda interviewed Merloyd for this book.

Q: What do you look for in a memoir?

First, a voice that is one of a kind. Also a life that arouses curiosity, because it could bring readers into a scene or society we don't know. Beyond that, a memoir might stand out because the person made a big change in the world, or because the writer is startlingly candid or funny about everyday little upsets and strivings.

Q: What kind of lives do you most want to read about?

Lives that make me realize there are other worlds out there, other ways to live. The many memoirs about celebrity lives that are already splattered all over, or those that try to blame all the writer's problems on parents, are among those I'd stay away from.

Q: When you edit a memoir, what is the most difficult thing you have to do?

The stage at the beginning when an author might be seeking the right approach, the right shape for the memoir, is where I feel I should be very careful. I worry about disrupting the ideas taking shape or suggesting a misguided path.

Q: What do you most enjoy about working with memoir?

Learning about these other worlds. Also the close conversations (closer than other kinds of nonfiction) about what matters to the writer in the most personal way.

Q: You edited the lovely memoir *When I Was Puerto Rican*. Can you tell us a story about that?

Esmeralda [Santiago]'s voice leapt out in a piece that she wrote about her mother, who supported eleven children by working in a bra factory (in the days when more privileged women were threatening to burn them). Her piece was called "Mami Wanted to Work," and I asked her if she wanted to keep going with it and write a memoir. She protested that she was too young to write a memoir, but I had the sense that she already had enough to fill several. And indeed, her story is now three books, *When I Was Puerto Rican* and *Almost a Woman* and *The Turkish Lover*. If we are lucky, there will be more.

Q: You also edited my memoir. Can you tell a story about that?

All your work about marine mammals was very impressive to me, and when Sarah Jane gave me the chance to consider publishing *I Want to Be Left Behind*, that work and the so-perfect title of this one grabbed my attention right away. Then all the common connections we had with other writers, and concern about the lives of animals and the way fundamentalists look right past them and all the rest of the natural world, made me grateful that I was given this chance. I'd worked with Sandra Steingraber, who wrote *Raising Elijah* and [*Living Downstream*], who also combines wonderful writing with deep environmental concerns, so your book just seemed to be a gem for my list.

Q: What do you learn from editing and reading memoir?

For a number of years I worked as a translator, and in editing and translating you keep trying to hear what the author most wants to say. With memoir that job is even more intense. Memoirs also hammer home the useful awareness that there are many ways to face life.

Q: What advice do you have for aspiring memoirists?

As I mentioned above, offering "advice" to an author about how to proceed is a risky business.

DOMINIQUE RACCAH

Born and raised in Paris before she immigrated to the United States, Dominique Raccah, the publisher of Sourcebooks, is an entrepreneurial leader in new forms of publishing. Considered a "maverick" by many in traditional publishing, Raccah has proven that close publisher-author bonds and being open to inventive publishing platforms can create successful books. Sourcebooks brings out three hundred titles a year, and many of its books are on the *New York Times* best-seller lists. Raccah was named FutureBook's Most Inspiring Digital Publishing Person of 2013. (See Chapter Notes, page 253, for a link to the Sourcebooks website.)

Q: What are your personal philosophies and passions when it comes to publishing?

Books change lives. Everything we're doing at Sourcebooks is really about that moment that we get to actually connect with readers. The truth about books is that it's one of the few times we allow other people into our heads. You spend so much time being who you are, distracted. But when you're reading, you allow that book to really seep into you; you interact with another's consciousness. It's total immersion.

Q: In a publishing world dominated by men at the top, Sourcebooks is the largest woman-owned trade book publisher in the country. Yet a recent Annenberg Public Policy Center survey cited that "women hold only 22 percent of the executive positions in top publishing companies." How do you think the female perspective has informed and guided you as a publisher?

It's really important that we're women-owned. Women are 65 percent of readers, 75 percent of buyers. We want to make sure that we serve them and understand their needs. That is real and inherent in all the work that we do. Uplifting and touching books serve the people. Digital doesn't scare me like others, because I am in service. If you think of publishing as a service—serving authors and readers—then you'll invent many ways of serving them.

Q: In your book, *Burning the Page*, author Jason Merkoski talks about the gender differences in those producing e-books, and says, "You have to ask yourself whether you trust these men (because they are mostly men—and mostly white men, at that). Do you trust them to make decisions for you on what books you're permitted to buy?" Do you also think women are at a disadvantage with e-book publishing?

Jason was one of the first Amazon.com evangelists. He is right that it's mostly white males who are making decisions about *all* of our culture. It's true in television, newspapers, and films, as well.

How does this work for younger women coming up? We need to give them a space and a vision to walk into a future. I'm surprised at how much publishing is the same since I started Sourcebooks in 1987. After all these years, I thought publishing would be different when it comes to gender equality. That's why new forms of publishing are so important now.

Q: You say you're "possessed" by the digital transformation of publishing. Sourcebooks is a leader in digital publishing and the promise of digital books. What about digital publishing energizes you—when other publishers are often confused or frightened?

The chance to touch more readers. Connecting authors to readers. One statistic haunts me: only about 5 percent of Americans go into bookstores in a year. Digital publishing is a chance to be mobile and reach every reader. With these new platforms, like our Put Me In The Story app, we can engage readers we might never have reached before. We want to make technology more accessible and create a world of readers.

Q: As a futurist yourself, can you imagine for us what books and publishing will look like in five years?

We'll see fewer publishers, more consolidation, and fewer literary agents. Barnes & Noble will still be around, as will independent bookstores. Print is a viable format for the foreseeable future. But the expansion of mobile is breathtaking. Look for new ways of enhancing e-books that will be very popular and intriguing to a new world of digital readers. I'm deeply engaged in the transformation of the book. (See Chapter Notes, page 253, for a link to her slide show, "The Book in Transformation" and for her Tedx talk, "The Promise of Digital Books.")

Q: Sourcebooks is having incredibly successful years, what you call an "amazing ride." In many of your online keynotes, you've mentioned that ever since the IPad debuted, that's how you read. How have digital books changed your own reading and publishing experience?

Reading on my iPad has done two things: one good and one not so good. I read more broadly than ever before. Yesterday I downloaded a book I might never have seen. I also read more distractedly, because on the iPad, I often leave off reading the book. So there's a loss in attention span.

Q: At a recent book conference, I listened to a panel of editors—even the young ones—declaring themselves "gatekeepers." Do you see yourself more as a "One Who Opens the Gates" to reading?

This arrogance in publishing costs us. As an industry, we need to be thinking more deeply about being open and getting feedback from our readers. That's why I love social media and I'm very active in online communities—who know me only by my Twitter handle—@draccah.

In publishing, too often the "gatekeepers" are keeping out people who don't have platforms—Twitter, Facebook, etc. Publishers should *create* that platform for the author. The conversation should not be about who to keep out, but how to include more voices.

Q: Sourcebooks' publishing partnership with authors seems very devoted and creates that successful "long tail" over time for authors. Do your offers of multibook deals with authors create author loyalty? And how does that benefit Sourcebooks?

Books don't happen in a vacuum. It takes a large community. For an author, the book may not work the first time, but maybe the third book breaks out. You've got to be loyal to authors over time. It takes a village, and it takes awhile. It really takes time to discover and "grok" what an author is doing.

Our authors have been diligent, and they work hard. As I just said at a conference about an author whose new book is finally breaking out: *Discover the gift that she is.* That's how we serve authors and readers.

Q: You said you change your mission statement frequently. What is it now?

One of our mission statements read: *We publish authors, not books.* I want to make sure the people I work for, authors, feel taken care of by their publisher.

18.
BOOK CRITICS

CLAIRE DEDERER

Claire Dederer is a well-known journalist and a book critic for the *Nation* and the *New York Times*, among other publications; she is also author of the best-selling memoir *Poser: My Life in Twenty-Three Yoga Poses*. (See Chapter Notes, page 253, for a link to Claire Dederer's website.)

Q: You've said that publishing a book doesn't change your life, but does writing memoir change you in some deeper way that has nothing to do with publication?

It sounds cheesy, but writing a memoir made me see firsthand the power of honesty. There were a lot of parts of my book that felt really squinchy to write—parts where I appear at my worst, and a very bad, embarrassing worst it is, too. It was really difficult to write those parts, but they're the bits that readers always say they love the best. Better than that: those are the parts that give readers the solace and comfort of knowing they're not alone in their own badness or suffering. If memoir is to be better than mere narcissism, this is the job it must do. The writer must be as clear and un-self-pitying and honest as possible; this is her act of generosity to the reader.

That certainly holds true in day-to-day life, where I've come to see that when I'm honest (but not, you know, a drag) with other people about my difficulties, rather than pretending everything is easy, we both end up feeling less alone. I think this has made me a better mother and friend.

Q: Your first memoir was a best seller. How does this affect writing your new memoir?

I can't complain about having written a best seller. *Poser* went out in the world and had a good life and for that I'm grateful unto abjection. That said, writing a second memoir is extraordinarily difficult. I think it would be difficult if twenty people had read my first book, or none, or a million. I was one of those people who foolishly, foolishly thought to myself, *Gee, my second book will be easy because I'll have done it once already.* I need hardly say: not the case. The work that goes into a first memoir is in some ways invisible, even to the author. You've been collecting material and writing it up for years or even decades, and you can just sort of cull it all for that first book. Then you mistakenly tell yourself you wrote the thing in one or two years or whatever, when in reality you've been writing it your whole life. With the second book, you have no such trove to plunder.

Q: As a book reviewer, what do you look for in a good memoir?

I look for books that are written in scene. Where the writer drags me by the hair into his or her life by delving deeply and funnily and with great detail into specific situations. To me, phrases like "We always used to . . ." or "We would . . ." are the death of good writing. Just tell me one specific situation and trust that as a reader I can extrapolate from there.

I also really love memoirs that reach, topically, beyond the author. That might mean the book is ostensibly about another person, or it might be about a specific circumscribed subject matter. Some examples: Geoff Dyer's *Out of Sheer Rage* starts out with his slightly bonkers obsession with D. H. Lawrence and ends up a very intimate self-portrait of Dyer himself. Nick Hornby's *Fever Pitch*, is ostensibly about soccer but is really about his parents' divorce. Lavinia Greenlaw's *The Importance of Music to Girls*, organizes a coming-of-age story around her favorite songs. Calvin Trillin's *About Alice*, a memoir of his wife, is really a self-portrait of the writer as husband. Laurie Colwin's *Home Cooking* books are about food, but also give a rich picture of her domestic life.

Q: How do you critique a memoir as opposed to a novel?

There's not really a difference. In both cases, I'm looking for great writing, of course, as well as an immersive reading experience and some indication that the writer understands the larger issues raised by his or her story.

Q: What advice can you give aspiring memoirists?

The main thing is to trust that your life is interesting if you write it well enough and are really honest about it. I devour memoirs of ordinary life; lots of people do. But aspiring memoirists are often afraid that the details of their lives are not inherently interesting. In fact, just the opposite is true: it's the specific intimate details of your life that will make your memoir not just a good read, but also important and beautiful and true and all the things we want literature to be.

DONNA SEAMAN

Since 1990, Donna Seaman has been a well-known editor and critic for *Booklist*, published in Chicago by the American Library Association. Seaman is also a frequent reviewer for the *Chicago Tribune* and the *Los Angeles Times*, and a guest editor for the literary magazines, *TriQuarterly* and *Creative Nonfiction*. The recipient of many awards for her literary criticism, Seaman's *Open Books Radio* is a must-listen for aspiring authors. Some of her interviews are collected in *Writers on the Air: Conversations about Books*, which the *Chicago Tribune* hailed as a "trove of insights into the creative processes and cultural observations" of diverse writers. (See Chapter Notes, page 253, for associated web links.)

Q: As a book critic, what do you most look for in a memoir?

The first thing I hope for is that the writer is telling her story with an eye to the larger world. If you're going to write, especially memoir, you must see yourself in a greater context. I seek out writers who see life whole, who are curious about the interconnectivity and complexity of existence, and who care, deeply and unabashedly, about the world.

Q: What is it about memoir as a genre that most intrigues you?

I've always been fascinated by and hungry for personal stories. Your curiosity about your life has to be about how you fit in with the rest of the world—the making of your "self." What are the conflicts that made you curious about things?

Good writing is a tonic. The work of inquisitive, imaginative, unfettered, and courageous observers, thinkers, and dreamers, provides succor. Heat and light. Food for thought and balm for pain. Lucid and compassionate literature breaks the isolating fever of the self.

Q: As a guest editor for *TriQuarterly*, you chose the theme "Strong Medicine." Do you see writing as healing?

Medicine, the dictionary tells us, is not only a "substance or preparation used in treating disease." It is also "something that affects well-being," and "magical power or a magical rite." The stories we tell alert us to our maladies and suggest modes of healing.

I found books healing because I discovered myself in them. *Little Women*, I was crazy for it. Loved Jo. Loved Dickens for his compassion. When I read Cheever and books by men, it really helped me get a grasp of other people's minds, which are always so mysterious. Without stories, we would have no clue to what goes on in the minds of others, no insight into how other people live and define life.

Q: What kind of lives do you want to read about?

Interesting question. Any kind of life. I'm drawn to lives of creative people and endlessly fascinated by artists and scientists. My mother is an artist, and my father an electrical engineer. So my father loves process and logic, binary system; my mother is all about beauty. She founded an artist co-op.

I had a younger sister, Claudia, who died when we were in our twenties. She was a poet, a really good one. Her death made me realize that literature was truly there for me. It was a terrible test case—can your passion really help you? But it taught me that art *can* sustain us. Books really do heal and strengthen us.

My sister and I shared a love of books. She was a mystic; I was practical. I used to demand that she give me copies of her poems. Even then, I was a little critic. As a girl, I kept lists of books I'd read. And they were long. So when I grew up to discover *Booklist*, it was as if the magazine was made for me.

Q: As a reviewer, why are you so devoted to the natural world?

I understood that the story unfolding around us in the living world is *the* story we need to know to survive. Nature writing is the greatest genre. The first poems were about the earth. All the great myths and sacred texts center on how we fit into our home, our habitat. How do you move on the earth and nurture the natural world?

As a girl, I was afraid of the damage done to the earth. It offended, appalled, and terrified me. I felt this would damage my life. Then I discovered [Henry David] Thoreau and Rachel Carson. Being able to

> *"Writing a memoir made me see firsthand the power of honesty."*
>
> —CLAIRE DEDERER,
> *POSER: MY LIFE IN TWENTY-THREE POSES*

explain what I was seeing when I looked at an ocean or a tree, made me a better earthling. It made me more careful and respectful. I'm so grateful when I come across good nature writing. I feel restored. The more we don't look at the living world around us, the more we destroy it. Writing about nature helps us see and connect to it again.

Q: When you review a memoir, what is the most difficult thing you have to do?

To separate the author and the narrator. To write about it as a book, not a critique of the memoirist. The process itself is so intimate, especially a memoir. You really feel you are in the confidence of this writer. It's a communion. You're spending hours with someone. Readers become experts on a memoirist's life and feel they truly know you. It's a very powerful connection.

Q: How do you think a memoirist should deal with issues of privacy, different points of view, and avoiding the one-note samba of unprocessed pain?

A tricky discussion! I believe that it takes a lot of chutzpah to write a memoir about people who are still around. It's necessary and legitimate. Each writer has to take responsibility for that. Don't censor yourself. But be realistic. Each person has to resolve that individually. I'm sure it's agony and scary for some people. I respect that. I don't respect sensationalizing or exploiting one's life. There are many creative nonfiction techniques for memoir that are controversial, but which I understand and embrace. Like dialogue. I'm assuming that the book as a whole is respectful of truth and clearly personal: "This is my version and only my version," I accept all of that because a writer is telling an *emotional truth*.

Memoir is more a story of the interpretation of your memories. They're not going to match anyone else's. You don't have to apologize for that. But you still have to set it in factual context.

Q: How do you envision traditional publishing five years from now?

E-books will be routine and established, but people will still want print books, because that's the best way to read certain kinds of writing. I see the big book publishers consolidating again and small presses flourishing. Publishing has never made any business sense. But a book is such great invention. It's a perfect object. We don't give things up. We have candles. And computers. Old-fashioned things, and also cell phones, bicycles, and cars. We keep everything. We still have buttons even though we have Velcro. We are greedy creatures. I like the integrity of an actual book. Print books calibrate your brain.

Q: What advice do you have to give to memoirists?

To write as well as you can. To invest as much feeling as you can. Be generous. Go as deeply into your life as you can. Good writing makes an ordinary life rich and interesting. It's great to write for yourself, but if you want to publish, you have to reach further. Therapy is fine, but the art of it—that's the best. That's where it becomes something other people want to read.

NOTE: Donna Seaman has set up a fund and an award for young writers, in memory of her sister, in partnership with the student-run literary magazine *Polyphony H.S.* (See Chapter Notes, page 253, for a link to the website.)

19.
MEMOIRISTS

DAWN RAFFEL

Editor and author Dawn Raffel was known for fiction—*Further Adventures in the Restless Universe*; *In the Year of Long Division*; and *Carrying the Body*—before her highly acclaimed illustrated memoir came out, *The Secret Life of Objects*. She was the Executive Articles Editor at *O, The Oprah Magazine* and an Editor-at-Large at *More* magazine, and she is currently Books Editor at *Reader's Digest*. (See Chapter Notes, page 253, for Dawn Raffel's website and the backstory about her memoir, first published on the blog of author Caroline Leavitt.) Brenda interviewed Dawn for this book.

The Accidental Memoir

I never intended to write a memoir. I'm a novelist and short story writer, and I was procrastinating on a novel when *The Secret Life of Objects* popped into my head, pretty much whole. What happened was this: I was drinking coffee out of the mug that I always drink from, despite having a cabinet full of mugs, because this one came from my mother's house, and for me it holds a hidden story about my mother and my aunt. I started thinking about this mug—you wouldn't give me five bucks for it, but to me it's priceless—and about the fact that I have a house full of objects like this. My possessions seem to hold some intangible residue of the places I've been and the people I've loved, and together they tell my life story. I sat down and wrote it all down as fast as I could—no mulling, so stalling, no second-guessing, no dying a thousand deaths over every sentence.

Normally, I need quiet to write, but my house was under construction and my kids were underfoot, and it didn't matter. A missile could have come through the wall, and I'd have simply ignored it. Normally, I freak out at around the three-quarter mark ("The Wall"), convinced the whole enterprise is doomed before I finally find a way to move forward. Not this time: The entire first draft was done in a week. This was, bar none, the most exhilarating experience I've ever had as a writer: a book that all but wrote itself. Yes, there was a lot of cleanup later, but cleanup is the easy part.

Will I get this lucky again? I sincerely doubt it. The aforementioned novel is still kicking my butt and threatens mutiny. But I think it's lucky accidents—whether whole books or a single syllable—and our willingness to accept them, that keep us in the game. The stuff we can't plan for, the surprises hiding in our psyches, at the edges of our consciousness is, for me, the sweetest part of writing.

Q: What do you look for in memoir?

I look for authenticity, honesty, and a sense that something is at stake. I also look for points of connection. Perhaps the hardest thing about writing a memoir is to be specific and precise without having the work become too narrowly personal. A good memoir invites the reader to consider his or her own life.

Q: What kind of lives do you most want to read and write about?

I often enjoy reading about what might be called "ordinary" lives, because no life is really "ordinary." I believe it was Isaac Bashevis Singer who said that even a pauper is a millionaire in feelings. There's a little bit of a vogue for memoir about extreme dysfunction—often, it seems, for shock value. I'm less interested in that. An intelligent, insightful look at a turning point in a quieter life suits me fine. I also like reading about adventure, whether that's adventure travel or intellectual or spiritual adventure.

Q: When you edit memoir, what is the most difficult thing you have to do?

I'm not sure there is a one-size-fits-all answer for that. Sometimes the issues are structural (the author knows so much that it is hard to organize). Sometimes there's an issue of editing down details that aren't resonant. And sometimes it's a matter of tone—avoiding the sense that the author is complaining or seeking revenge, which becomes wearying to read. Finally, sometimes the author needs more time, more perspective. For instance, if you are writing about a devastating loss, the act of writing might be cathartic, but it's likely that you will need a few years' perspective to create a memoir that will have significance to others.

Q: What do you most enjoy about working and writing memoir?

I'm endlessly fascinated by other people's lives!

Q: What do you learn from editing and writing memoir?

Any time you are writing well, whether fiction or nonfiction, you discover things about yourself that you didn't know, at least consciously. What emerges on the page is surprising. Editing memoir opens a window onto another life and also almost invariably broadens your understanding of storytelling.

Q: Any advice for aspiring memoirists?

You can be honest *and* kind. Treat all of your "characters" with respect. That goes for fiction, too.

> *"Lucky accidents and our willingness to accept them . . . keep us in the game."*
>
> —DAWN RAFFEL, *THE SECRET LIFE OF OBJECTS*

STACY HORN

Stacy Horn is a New York City journalist, NPR contributor, and author of the memoirs *Waiting for My Cats to Die: A Morbid Memoir* and *Imperfect Harmony: Finding Happiness Singing with Others* (See Chapter Notes, page 253, for a link to Stacy Horn's website.) Brenda interviewed Stacy for this book.

Q: How did writing *Imperfect Harmony* change or illuminate your life? Give us an example, please.

The message of the book is this: sing in a choir; it's one of the dependable routes to happiness that we have. In order to show that, for the two years it took me to write this book I was in a constant state of hypervigilance, always on the lookout for moments of happiness while singing. Then I'd take a deep breath and dive deep into those moments, making note of every nuance, every thought, every heartbeat, so I could go home and write about it all later.

As a result, to this day I can go back to any of them like a flashback—not just remembering them but reliving them. I'm in a section of Verdi's *Requiem* now, in a darkened church, feeling a little nervous that my voice isn't quite up to the beauty of the soprano to my left or the alto to my right, but I'm reveling in the harmony we're creating. The blend is perfect, we're shimmering, and John Maclay, our director, is looking at us like he doesn't have a care in the world.

Q: Did you listen to music as you wrote? What did you listen to?

No. I need quiet to write, except for the sound of birds, cars, trucks, and jackhammers outside my window, which after many years of city living are "nature" sounds to me now, and are soothing.

Q: Has singing so much of your life been a health benefit to you personally? You cite much research on this. Can you tell a story about singing and healing yourself?

I'd like to give an example of emotional healing. One year, in the space of a few months, my mother died, my cat died, and yet another relationship ended. I was singing the Brahms *Requiem* when we got to the line "Aber des Herrn Wort bleibet in Ewigkeit," which translates to "Yet the word of the Lord speaks for all time."

I'm agnostic, so strictly speaking, I don't know if there is a Lord or if his word lives forever. But when you sing, as opposed to listen, you become what you sing. So I *became* Brahms's *Requiem*. Brahms wrote a musical line to communicate forever and the possibility that death is not the end, and when I sang it, I felt it and believed it. It's an extremely triumphant moment in the piece. It surged through me from head to toe, transforming my grief to the hope that bursts forth in those measures. From that day forward, every day I felt a little better.

Q: When we write about real people in our lives, sometimes they have odd reactions. What was the response to this memoir from your director and other members of the choir?

If any of them are unhappy with it, they are keeping it to themselves, thank God. Instead, I'm hearing things like "I am burning right through it in utter joy," and "My eyes welled up many a time," and "OMG, it's *exactly* my experience to a T!"

Q: As a mezzo-soprano, I adored your discovery of singing rich harmonies. Can you talk about how seeking harmony and "the blend" affect other elements of your life?

I live my life the way I sing, going back and forth between the first- and second-soprano voice parts. Sometimes I do what I can to make sure my voice stands out on top, like a first soprano. But more often I go for the middle, where my voice is one of many. This is where I prefer to be. Maybe it's not such a good idea professionally, but like singing, it's a lot more fun in the middle. You don't feel the harmony as much on top, and the harmonies are the best part both in life and in singing. That said, the top feels pretty damned good at times. It's wonderful to have opportunities to sing, or live, both.

Q: When you wrote this memoir, did you feel a little uneasy talking about yourself after your more reportorial books?

This is how I felt on my pub date: Now whoever reads my book will know just what a loser I am. That's it, the jig is up, never leave your apartment again. The only thing that makes that okay is when people write to thank me for mirroring their own experiences. They're not losers, so maybe I'm not either.

Q: The weave of memoir and reporting in this book is seamless and beautifully conceived. One of my favorites is in the chapter "Toward the Unknown Region" when you move between Ralph Vaughan Williams's life and music, your own obsession with death, and the assertion that "death is among every choir's greatest hits." Then you end with the poignant piece on the pigeon. Was it difficult achieving this blend of memoir and reportage?

I have worked my entire writing life to be able to jump around like that. This is how my mind works, ricocheting from thought to thought to thought. Doesn't everybody's? It only took a few decades of tinkering to find a way to piece together the seemingly nonlinear storylines inside my head. Piece of cake.

Q: Are you gratified to see such a wonderful response—including a TEDx talk—to your book? How does this help you as a singer and a writer?

I've had people write me to tell me they've sung near me and my voice isn't bad. Can that be true? As a writer, it makes me think I might be up to the challenge of more books.

20.
HANDLING REJECTION

Ah, rejection—the occupational hazard for any real writer, our red badges of courage, our obstacle courses, and sometimes our teachers. How many careers (other than acting) offer the chance of such frequent rejection slips from total strangers, criticizing and ultimately "passing" on what you've worked so very hard to create? When you come to this final stage of publishing, you may have relied upon your skill and courage. But now we ask you to add one more element: stamina.

When you write a book, you're in it for the long haul. Most of all, you must believe that your life story is worthy and ready to be told to a larger audience than just family and friends. This takes not only some chutzpah, but also a strategy for surviving rejection if you are submitting to traditional publishers—and for handling bad reviews or criticism, even if you are self-publishing.

As writer and agent, we know firsthand about rejection in publishing. Every book we've ever sold has also been rejected. It takes only one publisher out of the many to whom your book is submitted to see the value of your work. Ask any of the famous writers who survived withering rejections—like Gertrude Stein, who received this rejection note that mocked her style:

Dear Madam,

I am only one, only one, only one. Only one being, one at the same time. Not two, not three, only one. Only one life to live, only sixty minutes in one hour. Only one pair of eyes. Only one brain. Only one being. Being only one, having only one pair of eyes, having only one time, having only one life, I cannot read your M.S. three or four times. Not even one time. Only one look, only one look is enough. Hardly one copy would sell here. Hardly one. Hardly one.

Sincerely Yours,
A. C. Fifield

The letter appeared in the *Atlantic*'s bracing and darkly funny feature "Famous Authors' Harshest Rejection Letters," which also showcased rejection notes sent to such literary luminaries as Ursula Le Guin for *The Left Hand of Darkness* ("unreadable . . . dry and airless"), Jack Kerouac for *On the Road* ("badly misdirected talent"), Peter Matthiessen for *Signs of Winter* ("adolescent, banal, self-pitying, trivial and totally unsympathetic") and Sylvia Plath for *The Bell Jar* ("there certainly isn't enough genuine talent for us to take notice"). (See Chapter Notes, page 253, for a web link to the article.)

As creative artists, we often must endure years of such rejections before someone takes notice. Much like actors, who are masters of weathering rejections, writers need to develop a kind of unquenchable optimism that keeps them knocking on doors—until finally, one of those doors opens. Sarah Jane's friend and actor, Cynthia Adler, says that the way you handle rejection depends to some extent on early family dynamics and also on whether or not you learn to be resilient. As a child, were you accepted, loved, and encouraged—no matter what? Did you grow up to have a strong inner core of well-being and self-worth? If not, has life taught you to be courageous and not to give up? "Persistence is everything," Cynthia says.

Another of Sarah Jane's actor friends says that if you allow rejection to stop you, it becomes a self-fulfilling prophecy. Better to acquire a kind of fierceness and learn to take rejection as a challenge—to develop a "To hell with them!" and "I'll show them!" attitude.

Life is full of stumbling blocks, critics, and naysayers. Like an athlete navigating an obstacle course, keep your eye on finishing the course. If that is publication of your memoir, it doesn't matter how fast you finish, there is real joy and a sense of accomplishment in holding a book in your hands. Or, if it's an indie e-book, your iPad or Kindle.

YOU'LL NEVER KNOW WHY

Here are a few tips to help you handle the inevitable rejection or criticism that comes as part of this process. First, give up trying to know why any traditional publisher rejects your book. Some writers have covered entire rooms with the wallpaper collage of rejections, most of them form letters. When Brenda worked as an editorial assistant at the *New Yorker*, one of her jobs was to type up rejection letters to authors and their agents. It was very instructive for a young writer who herself was receiving rejections from literary magazines.

It was in those dingy, labyrinthine magazine offices on West Forty-Second Street that Brenda first realized *who* was doing the rejecting is often more important than *why*. If you receive a form letter, more often than not, your book has been read only by a "slush pile reader" or an entry-level "editorial assistant." At the *New Yorker*, those slush pile readers were often overwhelmed with submissions, bleary-eyed, and rather hopeless about ever

> *Ah, rejection—the occupational*
> *hazard for any real writer.*

"discovering" anybody. Every year Brenda saw the annual acceptance sheets for new writers. Almost without exception, every unknown writer without a literary agent who was accepted at the magazine was "by referral." This meant that a staff writer, editor, family member, distant cousin, roommate at Yale, etc., had recommended this unknown writer to an editor. As in many professions, "who you know" can play a major role.

If you receive a form letter with a tiny scrawled note at the bottom from an anonymous editor, take heart. This means that someone actually took the time to read your work and encourage you. If that note asks you to submit more work, hop on it. Personal notes from editors transform the writer from supplicant to invited guest. In publishing, especially, relationships between writers and editors are to be nourished and held in the highest esteem. Be courteous and responsive when an editor or agent takes time to engage with you personally.

Your gender, where you live, your education, and your previous publications all help determine whether you'll be accepted. Before you expect to get a book deal, you should have already published in magazines, literary journals, or newspapers. Book publishers are nervous about "virgin" writers who have no publishing credits to their name. That being said, editors also enjoy the acclaim of discovering the next new big thing. Even if all you've published is a lively blog, it's a plus, since you already have a website, published stories, and an online "platform" or presence.

Of course, it *is* possible to get published without any of these conditions. If your work captures something, and that something just so happens to land on the right editor's desk at exactly the right time, the editor might decide to take a chance. True, you might not be offered a large advance, but books by unknown authors do get published.

Don't start first with the big magazines like the *New Yorker*, the *Atlantic*, and *Harper's*. Or if you do, include them in a multiple submission along with other smaller, more accessible publications.

AGENTS GET REJECTED TOO

This idea of "you'll never know why" is also part of an agent's world. Editor rejections of submissions often fall into this same category. Why didn't an editor care for the work? Some common answers are: "It just won't work on my list." Or "We already have a book on that subject." Or "It didn't engage me enough . . . I wasn't sufficiently involved with the characters . . . I didn't fall in love with the voice . . . This just isn't for us." And when writers ask their agents to explain an editor's rejection, often the only answer an agent is left with is: "You'll never know why."

Obviously, the opposite side of rejection is acceptance. From an agent's perspective, the willingness to take on a book is an act of extraordinary commitment. Like doctors, lawyers, or psychiatrists, agents suddenly find themselves responsible for this vitally important part of someone else's life. The difference is that agents do not get paid a single penny unless they sell their client's book. Just as with an author writing "on spec," so an agent does all the advance work before any sale. In order to make that sale, an agent must read, evaluate, and often edit proposals; read and review and respond to sample chapters and full manuscripts; suggest changes to make a book stronger, develop a list of possible editors, write a convincing pitch letter, send out submissions to editors, and follow up several times—and then, along with the writer, keep their fingers crossed.

Sometimes a book sells for six figures. But more often, it sells for far, far less. At 15 percent of the author's advance, you do the math to figure out the agent's commission. And although payment can be dramatically different, the work is the same, and it can take several months, even years to develop a marketable book. For an agent, even rejecting a proposal is not done without thoughtful consideration. Sarah Jane's rejection note—because this is what she believes—says:

> We are sorry that we are unable to use your material. There are many reasons to decline a manuscript, so please do not consider this to be a judgment on the value of your work.
>
> Bear in mind that this is just one individual response in a highly subjective business. It could well be (and often is) that another reader will see immediate possibilities. Needless to say, you should not accept ours as the final word.
>
> We wish we could respond to everyone with a personal note, but the heavy volume of submissions makes it impossible to do so. Please be assured that your proposal was given careful personal consideration.

On the other hand, if you find yourself in the very happy position of your project being accepted by more than one agent, remember to be gracious—especially to the agent(s) you reject. After all, you never know. The day might come when the rejected agent is the one with whom you'll be working.

THREE STRIKES

Once you've secured an agent and your book is ready to be submitted, there is a tendency, both on the part of the agent as well as the writer (to whom this feels like enormous progress, after months of hard work) to send it out in as large a multiple submission as possible. Like spaghetti, you think some of it is likely to stick. The trouble is, it often doesn't. The better policy is to submit to only three or four editors at a time. You start, of course, with your first choices, or the "first tier," of submissions. That way, if you're rejected, you won't have burned all your bridges.

If all the rejections say the same thing, pay attention. As Sarah Jane advises, "If three people say you're drunk, sit down." This gives both you and your agent the opportunity to look at the rejections, consider them, and, if necessary, make changes to the manuscript. Always be willing to hone your skills and to evolve. Whether your book is accepted or not, you can produce something that you know is splendid.

Sometimes you can really learn from a rejection letter, especially if an editor or agent has taken the time to offer an in-depth critique or if there is a consensus of editorial opinions. Brenda thinks of critiques as a chance to soar on the wings of an editor's suggestions. Good editing helps writers evolve.

Brenda also knew firsthand how heartbreaking and wrong-headed it could be when a would-be author didn't know how to interpret or work *with* rejection and editorial criticism. Brenda's mother, Janice, was a passionate journalism major who left the University of Colorado to marry and move to a remote forest lookout station in the High Sierra. The first sound Brenda remembers is that of her mother's fast and precise typing. Her mother's memoir, set in World War II, was a lively coming-of-age story about her work as a telegrapher for the Wabash Cannonball, while most of the men were away at war. Janice submitted her memoir, *All Aboard*, to New York City editors. She received several handwritten rejection letters—one even so encouraging that the editor passed along her memoir with a strong recommendation to a *Reader's Digest* editor. But she was so young, naive, and isolated from the publishing business, Janice didn't realize that she had been given an editorial invitation to the dance.

So Janice simply put her memoir away and resigned herself to writing long and engaging letters all her life. She had, in her words, "a baby instead of a book." That her baby, Brenda, has published books is a delight to Janice. But it doesn't change the fact that Janice was talented enough to have published herself—if only she'd known how to interpret and respond to rejection letters.

Publishing is often a very inscrutable business, even to those of us who have spent our lives in that arcane and sometimes confusing world. Educate yourself about publishing, which is changing drastically every day with new digital trends. There are many trustworthy bloggers who offer invaluable insights into traditional and indie publishing—ex-Knopf editor Jane Friedman's *Writing on the Ether*, and British blogger and best-selling author Joanna Penn's *The Creative Penn*. We also admire commentaries by Edward Nawotka, editor in chief of *Publishing Perspectives*, a leading online journal often called "The BBC of publishing." And of course, for traditional publishing news and cutting-edge information, read *Publishers Weekly*. (See Chapter Notes, page 253, for links to these sites.)

When you take your turn entering the twirling jump rope of traditional publishing, expect to trip. But then, consider your options, brush yourself off, and look for another way to skip in sync. Think of traditional publishing as a game of chance, good fortune, and who you know, and call upon your creative stamina. Remember, you never know.

But also remember that you wrote a book, and that is a real achievement. So take a moment and feel proud about what you've accomplished—and keep getting your work into the world.

21.
INDIE PUBLISHING

In this digital age there are many more options for publication than there used to be. Many "hybrid authors," like Brenda, publish both traditionally and independently, taking advantage of the higher royalties, artistic freedom, and more frequent publications that "indie" publishing, or self-publishing, offers. Brenda's students recently participated as a community in indie publishing, putting out a collection of their work, much of it memoir, in *Secret Histories: Stories of Courage, Risk, and Revelation.*

This chapter is adapted from articles, on both indie and traditional publishing, that Brenda originally published in the *Huffington Post.* We hope these help you decide on your publishing path. (See Chapter Notes, page 253, for web links to the original articles and an informative Mediabistro piece on publishing.)

AN AUTHOR'S GUIDE TO PUBLISHING

In the 1970s, when I was an editorial assistant at the *New Yorker* magazine—and getting many rejections—I used to fantasize about being my own publisher. "Give yourself a decade to finish a book," one of the revered *New Yorker* editors advised me. "Think of it as an author's apprenticeship."

After five years, I left the magazine and published my first novel, *River of Light*, with Alfred A. Knopf. To support my writing, I took a technical job as a typesetter so I could complete my working knowledge of books—from creation to editorial to production. I worked for decades as an editor and a writing teacher in universities and now teaching private classes. After publishing eighteen books with traditional houses—from Norton to HarperCollins to Penguin—I believed I was finally ready to become my own publisher. But there was still a stigma against the "vanity press" of self-publishing, no distribution, and little consumer demand.

I would have to wait until the twenty-first century when digital technology, direct distribution channels like Amazon, iBooks, and Nook, plus the popularity of inexpensive e-readers have finally made it possible for authors to become publishers. But journeying into self-publishing is like discovering a new territory with evolving rules. This is one of the most exciting and innovative times to be an author. Everything is in flux. Beloved librarian Nancy Pearl calls today's publishing scene "the Wild West of publishing."

My first task as a hybrid author was to bring back my out-of-print backlist—including *New York Times* "Notable Book of the Year" *Duck and Cover*, and *Animal Heart*—as e-books. In 2012 when I published my first YA novel, *The Drowning World* (in paperback and e-book editions), I carried many of my favorite professional book designers, editors, proofreaders, and marketing mavens with me into the indie world. I called this team my "publishing pod," in honor of the dolphin pods who have long inspired my nonfiction. Recently, *Publishers Weekly* featured *The Drowning World* and credited my expert team as "podmates."

Finding your publishing podmates—whether in traditional publishing houses or indie imprints—is the most important element of a successful book. Here are a few practical questions to help you decide whether to choose traditional or indie publishing, or both.

FIRST OR FOURTEENTH BOOK?

Are you a traditionally published author whose backlist is languishing with your publisher? Get the rights reverted to you and bring your backlist out again into e-books on all platforms. Smashwords and many other companies offer e-book conversion at a good rate. I used Data Conversion Library to convert my files into e-books on Nook, iBooks, Kindle, and Kobo. You can control your own pricing and track your own sales figures. If you have a literary agent, ask her to consider submitting your next book proposal to traditional houses while at the same time preparing it for indie publication. You may be delighted to have to choose between an offer and blazing your own indie trail— like Pulitzer Prize–winning author David Mamet, who in 2013, brought out his new indie book, *3 War Stories*, with the help of the Perseus Books–owned distributor, Argo Navis.

ADVANCES AND CROWDSOURCING

Traditional authors know that unless you're a celebrity or blockbuster author, advances have shrunk while Big Five publishers endure their current free fall. Some independent publishers are thriving, like Seattle's Sasquatch Books, with Nancy Pearl's best-selling Book Lust series. Or Algonquin Books of Chapel Hill, North Carolina, known for its literary panache with *Water for Elephants*. Or Sourcebooks, the largest female-owned publisher in America. Independent publishers offer modest advances. But they promise enduring support, not just for the launch and first few months; they have a select list of books and nurture all their authors over time. It's a smart business model that the Big Five publishers might find instructive.

Both traditional and indie authors can also turn to crowd-sourcing platforms like Kickstarter. To hire my expert traditional-publishing team, I raised more than $5,000 with my successful Kickstarter campaign, "Dive into the future in a sci-fi fantasy, *The Drowning World.*" It's best to make an engaging one-minute video and really pay attention to the rewards for your supporters. During my thirty days of raising funds on Kickstarter, it was thrilling to watch the sponsors come in—almost like being in Las Vegas on a winning streak. Kickstarter makes it really easy to keep updating your reader-sponsors, who are like a digital megaphone. Many of the thousands of visitors to my website each month find me via Kickstarter. Think of it as a pre–book tour to build your audience.

In the often solitary lives of authors, community is the hearth by which we warm ourselves.

E-BOOK—AND THEN PAPERBACK

Wait a few months after you publish an e-book and build your audience before publishing a paperback. Of course, there's Amazon's ubiquitous CreateSpace, iUniverse, and many companies that publish paperbacks for indie authors, especially as such giants as Penguin Random House get into the indie act. But why not also consider working directly with your local bookstore, if it's part of the very cool Espresso Book Machine (EBM) network, EspressNet, as I did with *The Drowning World.*

I published the paperback version using both EspressNet and CreateSpace. My favorite regional bookstores are Seattle's Elliott Bay Book Company, Third Place Books, and University Book

Store, and farther north in Bellingham, Village Books. *The Drowning World* is also on the fabulous Indie Bound international website, which makes it available for all independent bookstores to purchase.

Think of combining all of these publishing methods the way we now combine Western and alternative medicines. Or enjoying microbreweries and that special boutique as well as bigger department stores. Yes, EBM publishing is more expensive than CreateSpace or others, but it offers hands-on expert production, community, bookstore display, and public readings. According to the *Christian Science Monitor* and NPR, independent bookstores are making a comeback. Whether this is your first or fourteenth book, you may prefer the EBM's more collaborative and personal connection that authors always enjoy from actually meeting their publishers and loyal readers.

FIND EXPERTS AND COMMUNITY

You may also want to consider joining the Authors Guild or Independent Book Publishers Association (IBPA), a national organization that has clout and connections. Its annual IBPA Publishing University offers classes and keynotes with such luminaries as Guy Kawasaki, whose handbook *APE (Author, Publisher, Entrepreneur): How to Publish a Book* is indispensable. In addition, IBPA's "Ask the Experts" program lets indie authors learn about production, marketing, and social media.

In the often solitary lives of authors, community is the hearth by which we warm ourselves. It does take a village or a pod to publish a good book, whether with a traditional house or when independently launching into what Kawasaki calls "artisanal publishing."

Will the book business become more sustainable and egalitarian with the proliferation of e-books and self-publishing? A savvy editor at a recent panel on publishing trends commented, "Authors and readers now have many more options. Big publishers must be more flexible, nimble, and responsive." Like independent and small presses always have been.

Will big publishers now invest not just book by book, but instead in an author's whole body of work—supported and developed *over time*? It has always been difficult to get published by New York City houses, and it is even more difficult today. But now there are many new channels for authors to find readers—and they are not just respectable, but also sometimes profitable.

Will self-published authors develop their craft and practice rigorous revision, what one of my editors calls "the soul of genius," and employ the same expert editing and production standards of traditional presses? Or will we see a glut of unprocessed and unedited prose? Who will be the new gatekeepers that ensure quality control? Who will be the trusted reviewers, as newspapers and their book critics disappear? As we zoom into the future of books, will blogger-reviewers be sheriffs or outlaws?

In the next decade, who will be left standing at the O.K. Corral of book publishing? And will authors finally make a living wage with 70 percent royalties on self-published e-books? What is the book culture to become? Recently, the website BuzzFeed announced that it would publish only positive reviews of books—a trend?

We are now seeing the power shift from publishers to authors. Bowker, which issues ISBNs for books, reported that the number of self-published books rose by 59 percent between 2011 and 2013 (391,000 self-published books in 2012, with 40 percent of those, e-books). Indie publishing is the fastest-growing, most innovative, and accessible part of the swiftly tilting publishing industry.

Are we witnessing now a kind of Occupy Publishers' Row by enterprising authors? Or perhaps an Author Spring? Many predict that soon e-books will be the main revenue stream for authors and traditional publishers, with paperback and hardbacks demoted to subrights. This is a huge transition—as readers and authors are directly connected and the conversation continues online, the pages turning digital. Of course, there will always be a demand for print books. Smaller presses may flourish if they can keep their loyal readers and develop their own niches. Libraries are already lending e-books. Authors are now more at the center of it all.

Along with sharing power, authors also have to take more responsibility for what we create. We will have to learn how to find the best e-book formatters, so our books don't look amateurish and reveal subpar production values. This means employing cover designers, experienced editors, and proofreaders, and reaching out to our readers via social medias and blog tours. And let us never forget or forsake those independent bookstores who have valiantly kept authors alive and in touch with our readers.

With the upside-down of book publishing, authors and publishers are serving a new apprenticeship. And it won't take a decade. It's warp speed. But we still have to learn publishing all over again, from the bottom up. Laborious, yes. Daunting, yes. Exhilarating, yes. Authors and readers and publishers unite. Occupy the book!

EPILOGUE: YOUR STORIES WILL CHANGE YOU

The encounter with the creature changes the creator.

~C. G. JUNG

Both on the page and in life, you will not be quite the same person at the end of a memoir as at the beginning. If you publish, you also may be affected by your memoir's fate in the world—from instant success to respectful acclaim to total silence. But while publishing a memoir may not change your life, we believe that writing it will.

You'll change and grow as you fully realize and craft your life into story. It takes time to truly understand yourself and others. In 1980, when Brenda's beloved *New Yorker* fiction editor Rachel MacKenzie was dying from congestive heart failure, Brenda had a dream. Rachel entered her room with the unpretentious manner that was always her style.

"I've come to tell you that I'm in another place," Rachel said in her quiet, rather scholarly voice. "And I want you to know that where I am, there is still suffering." Rachel hesitated, her black eyebrows raised, so in contrast to her silver-haired bun and large glasses. As always, there was a slight sense of fond bemusement in her eyes. "But my dear, here you understand *everything*."

As memoirists, we try to understand everything while we're still alive. And that understanding can lead to many life changes. Rigorous self-scrutiny in telling your story demands truthfulness and recognizing your own missteps or moral conflicts. None of us is perfect, and it is our flaws as well as our truths that make us sympathetic and reliable narrators. In her memoir, *The Ogallala Road*, Julene Bair struggled with land, a love affair, water rights, and "how to continue being myself and my father's daughter." When we asked her how writing her memoir changed her, Bair told us that writing her life story made her more honest.

"For a memoirist, there is no separation, really, between writing and life," she wrote. As she dealt with whether to maintain or sell a family farm, which like many on the American prairie was unsustainably draining aquifers for irrigation, Bair faced her own demons: greed vs. conservation ethics, her need for family approval vs. her identity as a strong, independent woman. "Finally, I was letting myself be fully known by my readers in all of my imperfections," she concludes. "And I was bringing myself to the frontier of my ethical development." Creating her memoir profoundly changed Bair's sense of self and home. Its subtitle shows this inner conflict—*A Memoir of Love and Reckoning*. Bair, like that biblical Jacob, wrestles with a fierce inner angel to ask for a blessing. Her memoir is that benediction for us all.

You will not be quite the same person at the end of a memoir as at the beginning.

A LIFE CHANGE IN REAL TIME

When Episcopal priest David Robert Anderson found that his "tightly controlled life" was collapsing and his faith faltering, he turned to memoir. He wrote, "the best way to know God is to know your own self. So self-discovery turns up the divine." His memoir, *Losing Your Faith, Finding Your Soul: The Passage to New*

Life When Old Beliefs Die, explores his first glimpse of mortality, stress in his marriage, a mother's death, and even a fire that burned his church to the ground. He told Sarah Jane, his agent, that his dark night of the soul and spiritual evolution was "both necessary and transformative."

When Sarah Jane asked him "How did writing your memoir impact your life?" he answered: "In order to write that book, I had to live it first. I had to endure the losses and stay with the experience—not flee the pain—until it yielded its wisdom. It was like living through a life change and writing about it in real time."

Author Mirabai Starr answered the question this way: "Writing clears a space through the jungle of thoughts and emotions. Often the writing feels like a sifting process, in which I'm uncovering jewels that lie buried inside the mound of circumstances." Starr teaches writing and interspiritual workshops in which she says she witnesses "the transformational power of writing to create beauty and wisdom at the heart of our deepest brokenness, outrageous adventures, and blessed ordinariness." Anderson's and Starr's books are two of the memoirs that remind us of one of our favorite haikus:

> *Barn's burned down,*
> *now I can see the moon.*
> ~MIZUTA MASAHIDE

YOU ARE NOT ALONE: FIND A WRITING COMMUNITY

When writing a memoir, give yourself time and seek community. If you reach out, others will embrace you. Before you reach out to readers who are strangers, find readers who are allies—many of whom are on the same journey of telling their life stories.

Go to readings at your local independent bookstores. Try writing classes at your community college or elsewhere in your town. Make connections with bloggers, who welcome the exciting give-and-take of avid readers and engaged writers. Take workshops with visiting or local writers to hone your craft and meet other writers. Finding a writing community will make you a better writer—and it might even make the solitary journey of memoir more fulfilling. As E. M. Forster wrote: "Only connect."

In our experience working with writers, we've seen that writing makes better (and happier) people, and better people make better writing. Writing can be a lonely and competitive business, but we haven't seen many books written in a vacuum. If you again read the acknowledgments section in almost any book, you will see many personal thank-yous in addition to the author's agent and editor. Writing teachers will be there, as will members of writing groups, professors, workshop participants, husbands and wives, and even mothers-in-law (those who might be very annoying relatives can be very astute readers).

Most every writer needs the support of a community to work through the writing process—a community that offers mentoring, constructive criticism, encouragement, useful input, and abiding support. And if you can't find an existing writing community where you live—start one of your own.

WRITING, READING, AND EMPATHY

Originally, humans relied on storytellers to comfort and inspire us, to help us change our lives and navigate a moral universe. Later, we turned to religious works and philosophy for insight, and ultimately to novels and memoirs for a deeper and more universal understanding of the world and ourselves. The enduring popularity of storytelling, in whatever form, shows us that we learn how to grow and change from learning about other people's lives. Stories can bypass dogma and politics and even cultural divides, engaging the reader's compassion.

According to an article in the *New York Times*, a recent New School psychology study concluded that reading "sensitive and lengthy explorations of people's lives . . . can lead to more empathy and understanding." Professor James Pennebaker, psychologist and author of *Writing to Heal* and *Opening Up: Healing Power of Expressing Emotions*, says that merely turning the events of our lives into language actually effects changes in our brain and our immune systems. Reading makes us more human and humane— and so does writing. (See Chapter Notes, page 253, for a web link to an article about this.)

No story has as much power to change you as the story you tell yourself about yourself. More than any other, this is the story that drives who you are and influences you every step of the way. As memoirist Sue Monk Kidd writes, "I think many people need, even require, a narrative version of their life. Writing memoir is, in some ways, a work of wholeness." When Nancy Pearl interviewed Brenda for *Book Lust*, she commented, "I don't think I really knew you until I read your memoir."

In many spiritual traditions, the teachers say that the main problem we humans have is being stuck in our story. But it's not the story that's wrong; it's our limited or unexplored version of it. If we see the story with new eyes, it frees us to change it.

It's not just telling a better story; it's living that more evolved story. And knowing that at every moment a better story is available. Moment by moment, you can transform your life—and your story. And then—us.

ACKNOWLEDGMENTS

BRENDA: While joining me on book tour for *I Want to Be Left Behind*, Sarah Jane also answered the fascinating audience questions about writing memoir—and this book was born. In my work, no one has given me more heartfelt encouragement, keen insights, or bracing honesty than Sarah Jane. I'm so grateful to my students who for two decades have supported our vibrant and story-sustaining writing community; and, as the Salish Sea Writers, has just published their own anthology, *Secret Histories: Stories of Courage, Risk, and Revelation*. I am so blessed with my chosen sisters—Rebecca Lisa Romanelli, who is my most trusted teacher in spirit, courage, and life skills; Tracey Conway, who gives such savvy and witty counsel; my musical muse, Dianochka Shvets, my enduring literary ally, Susan Biskeborn, and my long-time first reader, Vanessa Adams. I am so fortunate to count among my steadfast friends, some of the finest working editors— Maureen Michelson of New Sage Press, my *Living by Water* editor, Marlene Blessing, Linda Gunnarson, of Sierra Club Books. All my gratitude to my generous brother and life-long friend, Dana Mark, and his family: Renee, Charlotte, Courtney, Christina, and Katy, who teach me so much about the real language of love.

SARAH JANE: They say that writing a book is a solitary endeavor. But after finishing *Your Life is A Book*, I am more than aware that anything I've been able to accomplish has only been thanks to the kindness of others. I am grateful there are so many people to thank. Brenda Peterson is my generous co-author. Such is the respect we have for each other's individual skills that never during the writing of this book did we finish each other's sentences—instead, we complemented them. Steve, husband of how many years? You were my first reader and my truest literary friend. Whenever I faltered, you were there to encourage me. Thank you for always making sure I deleted those exclamation marks. (!) Darling Elisabeth, you have given me the opportunity to do what I have loved best—being your mother—and more recently, being Kerwin's mother-in-law. To all those who have taken my workshops over the years, your response was my inspiration for embarking on this book. I am honored to have been a guide on your journey. Gratitude to my family, friends, colleagues and clients for your kind and loving support.

How fortunate we are to have Gary Luke as our savvy, witty, and visionary editor and publisher. Thank you, Gary, for your elegant edits and charming notes. In this book-making, we certainly lucked out with our copy editor, Elizabeth Johnson. Meticulous, yet kind, your comments, instead of scaring us, often made us smile. Project editor, Michelle Hope Anderson, is an editorial delight; designers Briar Levit and Anna Goldstein are a visual dream team; our Sasquatch publicity and marketing mavens, Sarah Hanson, Lisa Hay, and Haley Stocking are devoted book people and true authors' allies. Profound appreciation to all who contributed insights and words of wisdom: Cynthia Adler, David Robert Anderson, Elisabeth Adduru, Susan Bloch, Margaret Combs, Claire Dederer, Mani Feniger, Jane Goodall, Mary-san Matsuda Gruenwald, Fae Hopping, Stacy Horn, Gail Hudson, Diane Johnson, Aglaia Kremezi, Merloyd Lawrence, Toinette Lippe, Jarvis J. Masters, Linda Trichter Metcalf, Susie Middleton, Sy Montgomery, Nancy O'Hara, Gianluigi Quentin, Dominique Raccah, Dawn Raffel, Teresa Rhyne, Sharn Rocco, Rosalie, Katharine Sands, Donna Seaman, Laura Shapiro, Jessica Sinsheimer, Lavinia Spalding, Mirabai Starr, Elizabeth Van Deventer, Su-Mei Yu.

To our readers—we hope that this book will be a trusted and loving companion along your path.

CHAPTER NOTES

PART 1

Chapter 3: Your World as a Writer

"A Conversation with Alice Walker," by Donna Seaman in *American Libraries* magazine: tinyurl.com/ConversationWithAliceWalker

Chapter 5: Showing Up: Creating a Character of the Self

New York Times, "This Is Your Life (And How You Tell It)," by Benedict Carey, May 22, 2007: tinyurl.com/NYTThisIsYourLife

An American Requiem: God, My Father, and the War That Came Between Us, by James Carroll, Houghton Mifflin, 1996. An excerpt was published by the *Atlantic* in April 1996 at this link: tinyurl.com/AmericanRequiemExcerpt

Nancy Pearl interviews Brenda Peterson on the *Book Lust* TV show: SeattleChannel.org/videos/video.asp?ID=3031103

New York Times magazine article, "The Brothers Wolff," by Francine Prose, Feb. 5, 1989: tinyurl.com/BrothersWolffNYT

Chapter 6: Where Am I?: A Sense of Place and Time

Link for "grid cells" article is *New York Times*, "A Sense of Where You Are," by James Gorman, Apr. 29, 2013: tinyurl.com/SenseOfWhereYouAre

Ancestry.com: Ancestry.com

Margaret Bourke-White photos: tinyurl.com/BourkeWhiteDepressionPhotos

Travelers' Tales: TravelersTales.com/

Chapter 9: The Music of Memoir: Finding Your Own Voice

NPR's *Talk of the Nation*, Daniel Levitin, Ari Shapiro, and Stacy Horn: tinyurl.com/ImperfectHarmony

Chapter 11: Spiritual Memoirs

Christian Science Monitor, "Moral Dilemmas":
tinyurl.com/MoralDilemmas

NPR's *This I Believe*: ThisIBelieve.org/top/

Chapter 12: The Truth, the Truth, and Nothing But?

The New Yorker, Jan. 25, 2010, "But Enough about Me" by
Daniel Mendelsohn: tinyurl.com/EnoughAboutMe

Mimi Schwartz: online link to *The Fourth Genre* PDF of "Memoir?
Fiction? Where's the Line?": tinyurl.com/FourthGenre

"The Site of Memory," Toni Morrison (in *Inventing the Truth*
hardback, pg. 113)

Chapter 13: "Foodoirs" and Feeding the Hungry Writer

Lost magazine "A la Recherche du Cheese Perdu," Brenda Peterson:
LostMag.com/issue39/cheese.php

Chapter 14: Your Legacy

New York Times, Aug. 5, 2013, "Dying with Dignity and the Final
Word on Her Life," by Michael Winerip:
tinyurl.com/NYTDyingWithDignity

Time magazine "How to Live Long": tinyurl.com/HowToLiveLong

PART 2

Chapter 15: Better Blogging

Publishing Perspectives: PublishingPerspectives.com

Mediabistro: MediaBistro.com; MediaBistro.com/GalleyCat/

Time magazine's "The 25 Best Bloggers, 2013 Edition":
tinyurl.com/2013BestBloggers

"Bloggers Are Not Writers," by Rebecca Thorman, Kontrary.com:
tinyurl.com/BloggersWriters

"Jenny Lawson, The Bloggess," "The 25 Best Bloggers, 2013 Edition," TIME.com: tinyurl.com/JennyLawsonBloggess

The Bloggess: TheBloggess.com

Hyperbole and a Half, Allie Brosh blog: HyperboleAndAHalf.blogspot.com

New York Times Sunday Book Review, "Writing Bytes," Oct. 31, 2013: tinyurl.com/NYTWritingBytes

Chapter 16: Agents

Orion magazine, "Saving Seals," Brenda's first chapter of memoir appeared originally here: tinyurl.com/SavingSeals

Margaret Combs's website: MargaretCombs.com

Chapter 17: Editors

Merloyd Lawrence books: tinyurl.com/MerloydLawrenceBooks

Sourcebooks: Sourcebooks.com

Online slide show: "The Book in Transformation," Dominique Raccah: tinyurl.com/BookInTransformation

Dominique Raccah Tedx talk on "The Promise of Digital Books": tinyurl.com/TedTalkDigitalBooks

Chapter 18: Book Critics

Claire Dederer's website: www.clairedederer.com

Donna Seaman has set up a fund and an award for young writers, in memory of her sister. *Polyphony H.S.*: PolyphonyHS.com/submit/claudia-ann-seaman-award

Booklist: BooklistOnline.com

Open Books Radio: OpenBooksRadio.org/about.htm

Link to *TriQuarterly* guest post with Donna Seaman: tinyurl.com/DonnaSeamanGuestPost

Donna Seaman's website: DonnaSeaman.com

Chapter 19: Memoirists

Dawn Raffel's website: DawnRaffel.com

Backstory of Dawn's memoir from author Caroline Leavitt's website: tinyurl.com/DawnRaffelMemoirBackStory

Stacy Horn's website. StacyHorn.com

Chapter 20: Handling Rejection

"Famous Authors' Harshest Rejection Letters," by Romy Oltuski, *Atlantic*, Nov. 18, 2011: tinyurl.com/AtlanticRejectionLetters

Chapter 21: Indie Publishing

"Occupy the Book: Is It Author Spring?" Brenda Peterson, Oct. 26, 2011, *Huffington Post*: tinyurl.com/OccupyTheBook

"An Author's Guide to Publishing," Brenda Peterson, *Huffington Post*, May 3, 2013: tinyurl.com/AuthorPublishingGuide

Mediabistro: "The Number of Self-Published Titles on the Market Up 59% Last Year: Bowker," Nov. 13, 2013: tinyurl.com/SelfPublishingReport

Edward Nawotka, "If Book, Then": IfBookThen.com/Edward-Nawotka-2/

Jane Friedman, *Writing on the Ether*: JaneFriedman.com

Joanna Penn, *The Creative Penn*: TheCreativePenn.com

Publisher's Weekly: PublishersWeekly.com

Epilogue: Your Stories Will Change You

"For Better Social Skills, Scientists Recommend a Little Chekhov," by Pam Belluck, *New York Times*, Oct. 3, 2013: tinyurl.com/NYTReadChekhov

RECOMMENDED MEMOIRS

While it would be impossible to list all the memoirs we love, here are a few of our favorites, some of which we've already mentioned in the text.

Classics:

In Search of Lost Time, Marcel Proust

The Diary of Anaïs Nin, Anaïs Nin

Family:

The End of the World as We Know It: Scenes from a Life, Robert Goolrick

Running in the Family, Michael Ondaatje

Dreams from My Father, Barack Obama

My Mother's House and Sido, Colette

Speak, Memory, Vladimir Nabokov

The Death of Santini and *My Reading Life*, Pat Conroy

Refuge: An Unnatural History of Family and Place, Terry Tempest Williams

A Tale of Love and Darkness, Amos Oz

Brother, I'm Dying, Edwidge Danticat

Living To Tell the Tale, Gabriel García Márquez

World War II:

An Interrupted Life: the Diaries of Etty Hillesum, Etty Hillesum

Seven Years in Tibet, Heinrich Harrer

Maus, Art Spiegelman

Vietnam:

The Things They Carried, Tim O'Brien

Humor:

Neither Here nor There: Travels in Europe, Bill Bryson

Mama Makes Up Her Mind: And Other Dangers of Southern Living, Bailey White

Animals as Family:

Pack of Two: The Intricate Bond between People and Dogs, Carolyn Knapp

Of Wolves and Men, Barry Lopez

Reason for Hope: A Spiritual Journey, Jane Goodall

Thinking in Pictures: My Life with Autism, Temple Grandin

Food and Travel:

My Life in France, Julia Child

On Persephone's Island: A Sicilian Journal, Mary Taylor Simeti

Travel:

The Olive Farm, Carol Drinkwater

A Thousand Days in Venice: An Unexpected Romance, Marlena de Blasi

Blue Highways: A Journey into America, William Least Heat-Moon

The Great Railway Bazaar, Paul Theroux

The Songlines (or any of his travel memoirs), Bruce Chatwin

Music:

The Inner Voice: The Making of a Singer, Renée Fleming

Just Kids, Patti Smith

Foodoirs:

The Tenth Muse: My Life in Food, Judith Jones

Kitchen Confidential, Anthony Bourdain

Fresh Off the Boat, Eddie Huang

Blood, Bones & Butter: The Inadvertent Education of a Reluctant Chef, Gabrielle Hamilton

Consider the Oyster (or anything by this author), M. F. K. Fisher

The Man Who Ate Everything, Jeffrey Steingarten

Big City, Tough Guy:

A Drinking Life, Pete Hamill

Townie, Andre Dubus III

The Boy Detective: A New York Childhood, Roger Rosenblatt

Spiritual:

Bones of the Master: A Journey to Secret Mongolia, George Crane

The Crosswicks Journals series, Madeleine L'Engle

Girl Meets God, Lauren F. Winner

The Cloister Walk, Kathleen Norris

My Land and My People, Dalai Lama

Nature:

Pilgrim at Tinker Creek, Annie Dillard

The Woman Who Watches Over the World, Linda Hogan

Among Flowers: A Walk in the Himalaya, Jamaica Kincaid

Cultivating Delight: A Natural History of My Garden, Diane Ackerman

Medical:

Complications: A Surgeon's Notes on an Imperfect Science, Atul Gawande

Confessions of a Knife, Richard Selzer

Friendship:

Truth & Beauty, Ann Patchett

The Soloist, Steve Lopez

Survival:

Strange Piece of Paradise, Terri Jentz

Hope Against Hope and *Hope Abandoned*, Nadezhda Mandelstam

Mother Memoirs:

Black Milk, Elif Shafak

Paula: A Memoir, Isabel Allende

Running Memoirs:

What I Talk About When I Talk About Running, Haruki Murakami

Art Memoirs:

Ai WeiWei Speaks, Ai WeiWei with Hans Ulrich Obrist

Writing Craft Books:

If You Want to Write, Brenda Ueland

Take Joy: A Writer's Guide to Loving the Craft, Jane Yolen